How do our brains enable us to speak creatively and build up an understanding of language? This concise and accessible book examines the linguistic and neuroanatomical underpinnings of language and considers how language skills can systematically break down in individuals with different types of brain structure, such as children with language disorders, adults with left- or right-hemisphere brain damage, demented patients, and people with reading problems.

In a wide-ranging discussion, the authors cover brain damage in bilingual people as well as the reading and writing difficulties experienced by dyslexics and dysgraphics. Information is also provided on "split-brain" patients, visual gestural languages, and language savants. By studying the linguistic behavior of these groups the authors provide an understanding of how language is organized in the brain.

Language and the Brain

Cambridge Approaches to Linguistics

General editor: Jean Aitchison, *Rupert Murdoch Professor of Language and Communication, University of Oxford*

In the past twenty-five years, linguistics – the systematic study of language – has expanded dramatically. Its findings are now of interest to psychologists, sociologists, philosophers, anthropologists, teachers, speech therapists and numerous others who have realized that language is of crucial importance in their life and work. But when newcomers try to discover more about the subject, a major problem faces them – the technical and often narrow nature of much writing about linguistics.

Cambridge Approaches to Linguistics is an attempt to solve this problem by presenting current findings in a lucid and non-technical way. Its object is twofold. First, it hopes to outline the "state of play" in key areas of the subject, concentrating on what is happening now, rather than on surveying the past. Secondly, it aims to provide links between branches of linguistics that are traditionally separate.

The series will give readers an understanding of the multi-faceted nature of language, and its central position in human affairs, as well as equipping those who wish to find out more about linguistics with a basis from which to read some of the more technical literature in textbooks and journals.

Also in the series

Forthcoming titles include

Language
and the Brain

LORAINE K. OBLER

City University of New York Graduate School

KRIS GJERLOW

Gamut Logistics, Elizabeth, New Jersey

CAMBRIDGE
UNIVERSITY PRESS

MidTown

PUBLISHED BY THE PRESS SYNDICATE OF THE UNIVERSITY OF CAMBRIDGE
The Pitt building, Trumpington Street, Cambridge CB2 1RP, United Kingdom

CAMBRIDGE UNIVERSITY PRESS
The Edinburgh Building, Cambridge CB2 2RU, UK
  http://www.cup.cam.ac.uk
40 West 20th Street, New York, NY 10011-4211, USA
  http://www.cup.org
10 Stamford Road, Oakleigh, Melbourne 3166, Australia

First published 1999

Printed in the United Kingdom at the University Press, Cambridge

Typeset in Photina 10/12 [VN]

A catalogue record for this book is available from the British Library

Library of Congress cataloguing in publication data

Obler, Loraine K.
Language and the brain / Loraine K. Obler, Kris Gjerlow.
    p.   cm. – (Cambridge approaches to linguistics)
Includes bibliographical references and index.
ISBN 0 521 46095 6 (hardback)   ISBN 0 521 46641 5 (paperback)
1. Biolinguistics.   2. Language disorders.   3. Brain damage.
I. Gjerlow, Kris.   II. Title.   III. Series.
P132.025   1998
401–dc21   97-47554 CIP

ISBN 0 521 46095 6 hardback
ISBN 0 521 46641 5 paperback

5/4/2000 Grad School of Ed + Psych

To Nathaniel David Fearey Obler LKO
In memory of R. M. R. Hall KG

Contents

Figures

Tables

Preface

The field of neurolinguistics – the study of language in the brain – has fascinated both of us from our early days in doctoral studies. Trained as linguists, we both were drawn from the beauties of abstract theorizing about language structure to the belief that the patterns, structures, and rules that languages manifest must be grounded, indeed, embodied in the brain.

Because the field of neurolinguistics weaves together many sources, we found ourselves exploring outward from language to the study of behavioral neurology, aphasiology, speech-language pathology, neuropsychology, and cognitive science, not only for the content of these fields but also for the research approaches each contributes to the study of neurolinguistics. This confrontation with different research paradigms relatively late in our intellectual training has been particularly stimulating, enabling us to appreciate the strengths of, and gaps in, linguistic methodology. The contrasts in research approach between the interdisciplinary field we were entering and the discipline we came from as students stimulated us to look back on the history of the new science. We view with wonder its periods of rapid grasping of knowledge alternating with periods of slower building on previous knowledge, then acceleration toward pointed debates about the unity or diversity of aphasia types, about the relative usefulness of case and group studies, about the character of apparent breakdown of syntax in brain-damaged patients with language disturbance.

Working with colleagues across a number of disciplines also challenged us to think about the special status we linguists accord to language among cognitive abilities while other scholars see language as one among many cognitive abilities. In this book we hope to share our enthusiasm for the field and spark readers' interest in its multiple facets as ours have been sparked.

Structuring a book on neurolinguistics is particularly difficult because the field is so multi-dimensional. A number of introductions to the field, or to aphasiology in particular, are structured around different aspects of language or language performance (e.g., phonology, morphology, syntax, writing disorders, etc.). Such structuring assumes a readership familiar with the populations of brain-damaged patients – particularly aphasics – from whom neurolinguistic data is collected. We assume that many readers of this volume will not have such background, and thus we choose to focus in the majority of the chapters on the special populations who provide us with knowledge of language organization in the brain. At the end of each chapter on a given population, we summarize what we can learn from that population about brain organization for language. Only in the penultimate chapter do we pull together all the information, gleaned from these different research populations, about the psychological reality of different linguistic phenomena and levels.

Because we assume our readers come from numerous disciplines, we provide a glossary at the end of the book with terms from linguistics, neurology, speech-language pathology, etc. Also, at the first mention of each term we provide a definition within the text. While we permit some redundancy to remain within the chapters, on the assumption that not all readers will read the book from beginning to end, we provide the glossary so that readers who may choose to dip into a later chapter before an earlier one can find the definitions they need without recourse to the index.

We consider ourselves fortunate to be living in a time when large numbers of women can both master an intellectual field and contribute to it independently, and we thank the women and men of recent generations who have made this possible. Thanks go to Kris Gjerlow's colleagues in the group at Kingsborough Community College, and Loraine K. Obler's, Feminist Research Methodology group for critical discussion over the years. Dana McDaniel, Ann Peters, Jean Aitchison, Judith Ayling, Sarah Williams, Martin Albert, Kenneth Hyltenstam and an anonymous reviewer have been generous in providing comments on earlier drafts of this book.

Loraine K. Obler and Kris Gjerlow

I appreciate the models Ernest Abdel-Massih, Margaret Fearey, and Michael Patrick O'Connor provided for how to be a productive scholar and intellectual. To Martin L. Albert I owe many thanks for engaging me in neurolinguistics, mentoring my first decade in it, sharing with me an appreciation for its history, and continuing to collaborate in our Language in the Aging Brain laboratory at the Boston Veterans Administration Medical Center. I have learned a lot from other members of our lab, most particularly Marjorie Nicholas, Lisa Connor, and Rhoda Au, as well as from colleagues at the Aphasia Research Center there. I consider myself most fortunate to have arrived there when Harold Goodglass, Norman Geschwind, and Edith Kaplan enriched us all with their individual ways of blending clinical brilliance and research expertise. The opportunity to work on research projects with Lise Menn, Jean Berko Gleason, and Harold Goodglass there was invaluable. Indeed the environment was so stimulating that many international scholars were drawn there; from among them Lise Menn and I formed the Cross-Language Agrammatism team whose work over the last decade and a half has shaped much of my thinking on agrammatism. Grants from the Veterans Administration, the National Institutes of Health, the National Science Foundation, and the CUNY Research Foundation have funded much of my research.

The opportunity to work in the Speech and Hearing Sciences Program of the City University of New York Graduate School has expanded my knowledge of neurolinguistics greatly, as teaching requires one to explore outside the narrower focus funded research demands. I have learned much about science, as well as about their individual fields respectively (namely, speech science and hearing science) from Katherine Harris and Arthur Boothroyd. My students in that program, as well as at Emerson College, have served as an additional source of continued learning for me. Mira Goral helped with editing and locating references. Melissa Bortz and Erika Levy commented helpfully on an earlier draft of this book and Erika helped proof it. Susan De Santi helped make the neuroanatomic figures more useful. Nancy Eng helped with references to Chinese and other tone languages. Elmera Goldberg provided examples of aphasic patients' productions. Cecelia Davidson provided useful references on children's language.

At the CUNY Graduate School, Loretta Walker's intelligent help in word-processing this manuscript (and many others) has been invaluable, as has that of Myrna Brasie in Boston. John Dyke, of the Medical Media Service of the Boston VA Medical Center, has contributed his artistry to the illustrations for this text. Michele Hudak and Sendia Kim have helped locate references, and Anna Mackay took responsibility for obtaining permissions.

Loraine K. Obler

We particularly want to thank the colleagues over the years who have contributed to our ability to be able to conceive and to realize a book such as this. I appreciate Bob Faraci and Bob Herbert whose undergraduate linguistics courses were the basis for my decision to do graduate work in linguistics. Each of them has a talent for presenting material in a clear and engaging manner.

In later years I learned much about linguistics and about being a scholar from Marilyn Gaddis-Rose, Bob Fiengo, Chuck Cairns, Helen Cairns, and Mike Hall. Their contributions to my intellectual development are invaluable.

I have also gained much in perspective from those who studied alongside me, especially Tom Maxfield and Dana McDaniel. My colleagues at Kingsborough Community College, especially Cindy Greenberg, Cliff Hesse, and Mary Crowley, gave generously of their time as "sounding-boards" for ideas I considered treating in this book. The single most important person in sparking my interest in neurolinguistics and mentoring me over the last six years is my co-author Loraine Obler. As she has done for many students, she provided an excellent example of dedication, intellectual curiosity, and enthusiasm. As we became colleagues, she continued to look out for me, providing me with information on research opportunities. I am truly grateful for her support.

Kris Gjerlow

1 Neurolinguistics

"Little words, no" is how one brain-damaged patient described his loss of language. Another whose comprehension of spoken and written languages was markedly worse than that of the first patient, reported "The small words are too big for me." We see from the form of their utterances as well as their content that these two patients are suffering from different types of language break-down.

What can their problems tell us about how the human brain permits us to speak and understand what others say? Study of such aphasic individuals – people whose brain damage has af-fected some or all of their language skills – has been at the core of neurolinguistics.

What is neurolinguistics?

Neurolinguistics, as its name implies, is the study of how the brain ("neuro") permits us to have language ("linguistics"). Neur-ologists study brain and nerve systems; those neurologists who contribute to the field of neurolinguistics study human neurology and how behavior breaks down after damage to the brain and nervous system. They might ask about the two patients mentioned above where precisely their brain damage lies. Linguists study the way human language is structured. Those linguists who contrib-ute to the field of neurolinguistics are interested in how language structures can be instantiated in the brain. They would observe that the first patient quoted above actually avoided using many of the "small words" one might have expected, yet included one ("no"), and ask why this is.

In fact neurolinguistics is such an interdisciplinary field that more disciplines contribute to it than those its name proclaims. Psychologists also participate in neurolinguistic study, especially psycholinguists (who study language processing in normal individuals) and neuropsychologists (who study the breakdown of cognitive abilities that result from brain damage). Psycholinguists are more likely to study language processing in normals than in patients with brain damage; they might ask how these "small words" that the patients report having problems with are heard and understood in the course of ongoing speech. Neuropsychologists will focus on brain-damaged patients – often those without aphasia – and may ask if people with damage to other areas of the brain that do not result in frank disturbance to language have any problems processing the "small words." If so, they may ask whether these problems may be linked to problems that are not, strictly speaking, language abilities, such as memory or attention.

Speech-language pathologists (professionals trained to provide therapy for language problems) contribute their special knowledge of aphasia and their clinical and theoretical approaches to language breakdown. They are likely to research the other language abilities of patients like the two cited above. Why are the "small words" processed when the patients must simply repeat them as single words, or in sentences? Can the patients read these words and understand them correctly? What sorts of speech-language therapy can help patients with these problems?

Cognitive scientists (scholars involved in studying of the processes involved in thinking and theories that may explain them) also have interests that overlap with those of neurolinguistics; they contribute to answering questions such as how short-term memory interacts in language processing. They also suggest ways of using computer modeling to understand language performance.

While the term "neurolinguistics" is relatively new, the field can be traced back to the nineteenth century. It was physicians who opened up the field with their observations of correlations between language disturbance resulting from brain damage and the particularities of the brain damage that resulted in it. One of these physicians, a nineteenth-century neurologist named Paul

Broca, recognized that a certain area on the left surface of the brain was responsible for language. He himself was an exemplar of interdisciplinary interests; he was involved in forming the Anthropological Society in Paris.

In that century, also, what we now call neurolinguistics was in the process of distinguishing itself from phrenology (the linking of human characteristics such as "amativeness" – presumably the ability to love – with the relative size of skull areas, discussed in chapter 3) and, a bit later, psychiatry, the study of mental illness.

In many ways, despite its roots in the nineteenth century, neurolinguistics must be seen as a relatively new science. It is new compared to sciences like physics and chemistry whose practitioners have carefully worked out a substantial fact base and generally accepted theories to explain the facts. Neurolinguistics has yet to develop a single large-scale unified theory acceptable to all – or even most – neurolinguists, no doubt in large part because none of the fields which contribute to it has developed a single, agreed-upon model. However, substantial elements of theories are available that explain clusters of phenomena. Workers in the field attempt to contribute descriptions of additional phenomena that will require theory to understand them, and theories – or at least models – to account for the phenomena already described.

The structure of this book

We assume readers of this book know somewhat more about language than they do about the brain, so the next chapter (chapter 2) provides an introduction to the brain structures that play a role in storing and processing language. (Relevant linguistic terms can be found in the glossary.) In chapter 3, we sketch out a number of the techniques that are used to study brain organization for language and discuss the notion of lateral dominance, the ability of one half (one hemisphere) of the brain to be substantially more involved in language processing than the other.

With chapter 4 we begin our presentation of neurolinguistic knowledge by focusing on one particularly concrete set of objects-of-study in the field of neurolinguistics, the various groups of individuals whose behavior provides clues to brain organization for language. As we mentioned in the preface, it is these groups that we have used to structure most of the rest of the book, so readers can see what sorts of information have been and can be gleaned from studies of each of them.

Aphasics – individuals like those cited at the beginning of this chapter who have suffered brain damage with the result that aspects of their language are impaired – were the first population to permit study of the systematic breakdown of language. From that breakdown we learn what the components of language are as they must be represented in the brain and processed by it. Because so much work has been done on aphasics' language, we have written two chapters on aphasia for this book, one focusing on the symptoms and syndromes as our interpretation of these has developed, and the second on the more modern linguistic understandings that derive from studying the phenomena of aphasia and attempting to elucidate theories to explain them. In these chapters we discuss types of questions that working with aphasics leads us to, questions like:

- If some aspects of language are impaired and others are not, what does that tell us about the way language is organized in the normal brain?
- If we see certain patterns of recovery from aphasia, what does that tell us about how the brain is organized for learning language and processing it?

Following the studies of aphasia in adults, we discuss childhood aphasia. In some ways, the sudden onset of language problems in childhood, due to brain damage, is similar to that of adulthood, but in other interesting ways it is different because both the brain and language of the child are still maturing, while those of the adult are more mature and stable. A study of such children permits us to discuss the notion of plasticity, that is, the way the brain can reorganize itself after damage, at least during childhood. Linked to "plasticity" is the notion of a critical period for language acquisition, that is a period, somewhere in childhood or at puberty, after which learning language becomes markedly more difficult. This difficulty arises, presumably, because of loss of the brain templates that we assume children are born with that permit them to learn language. Also lost over time is the possibility of creating many new connections among brain cells that make language acquisition easy in young children. We also consider the case of Genie, a modern-day "wild child," to learn what severe deprivation of language throughout childhood teaches us about brain organization for language and the critical period. In this chapter (chapter 6) we discuss people with language disorders that run in families because their performance on language tasks gives us hints about the ways the normal newborn's brain must be ordered for language processing to occur.

Aphasia in adults is virtually always the result of disturbances to what we call the "language area" of the brain, that is, the part of the brain that is crucial for many aspects of language; see Figure 1.1. The language area is relatively circumscribed in what we call the dominant, left hemisphere (dominant because for most humans language seems to rely more heavily on it). However, disturbances in language performance more broadly construed can be seen in patients with brain damage outside this language area. Most interesting of this group are patients whose brain damage is not to the so-called language "dominant" hemisphere but to the so-called "non-dominant" one, usually the right hemisphere. Thus we devote a chapter (chapter 7) to discussion of what we learn about language organization in the brain from study of this population whose core linguistic abilities (phonology, syntax, and, often, lexical access) appear quite spared, yet whose discourse and other pragmatic aspects of language are somewhat deviant. From right-brain-damaged patients we can ask how aspects of language other than the ones that linguists have traditionally thought of as core aspects can systematically break down with brain damage. From such studies we learn about the participation of the non-dominant hemisphere in pragmatic aspects of language performance among normals.

Wernicke – the next neurologist after Broca who moved our field forward – tussled with the relationship between language and thought in his classic 1874 paper where he described two fluent aphasics, one of whom, we maintain (Mathews, Obler, and Albert, 1994) was clearly demented. Alzheimer himself, the neurologist after whom the most common dementing disease in the Western

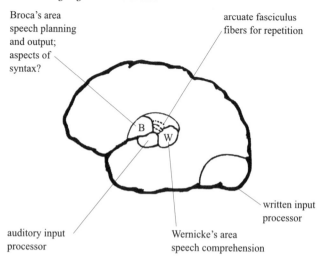

Figure 1.1 A modern schematic of the language area of the left hemisphere.

world is named, gave substantial attention in his papers early in the twentieth century to describing the language breakdown of patients with what we now call Alzheimer's dementia. Precisely because the various dementing diseases permit us to consider the ways in which language performance and abilities interact with other cognitive abilities, we have devoted a chapter (chapter 8) to what study of this population contributes to the field of neurolinguistics.

We have put into a separate chapter (chapter 9) the topic of individuals with disturbances of reading (dyslexics) and writing (dysgraphics) or spelling because the phenomena of written language are so different from those of oral language. Here we cover both those children for whom learning to read is particularly difficult and those adults whose brain damage has resulted in particular difficulties with reading. From dyslexics and dysgraphics we can learn the abstract components necessary for processing written language (i.e. reading or writing) in normals and glean further information about the way visual language systems are organized in the brain.

As with most of our sciences, in the early stages one must simplify, and thus relatively little mention was made in the first century of neurolinguistic science of the fact that many of the aphasic patients studied were bilingual or bidialectal. By the last decade of the nineteenth century, however, neurologists such as Pitres (1895) and Freud (1891) had expressed some interest in the questions of how the various languages of bilinguals or polyglots can break down and recover after brain damage. The last half of the twentieth century has seen an increase in studies of language organization in bilingualism which we detail in chapter 10. Focusing on bilingual individuals permits us to ask questions about how "modular" – i.e. independent – the organization is of similar materials that must be processed separately in the brain, and about how specific languages with specific structures may be differently organized relative to each other in the brain.

Of course many other smaller populations of individuals have provided us with substantial important knowledge about how language is organized in the brain, and we have found ways to include information about such individuals as "split-brain" patients (those patients in whom surgery has been done so that the left and right hemispheres of the brain no longer communicate with ease), speakers of visual-gestural language and language savants (those among a group that used to be called "idiots savants" whose special abilities are in language skills) in various of the chapters.

The objects of neurolinguistic study

The two objects of study that must be linked in neurolinguistics are language and neural components. Each of these can be divided, in principle, into actual permanent "things" that must be studied and the processes that these things engage in. In language the taxonomy of things-to-be-studied can be constructed in a number of ways. Linguists have traditionally considered a set of levels for analyzing language that may be more or less independent of each other: the sound system (phonology), the system of meaningful units underlying words (morphology), the system for combining these units into sentences (syntax), the system for combining the sentences into larger meaningful utterances (discourse), and the system for understanding meanings (semantics). Another useful classification scheme within linguistics for the purposes of neurolinguistics is the set of distinctions among different types of language. Relevant for our purposes here are the distinctions between oral and written modalities for language, and the distinction between oral and visual-gestural language. Also pertinent is the language typologists' distinction between languages that rely heavily on affixed markers to indicate morphosyntactic roles (highly synthetic languages like Finnish and Hungarian) as opposed to languages that require virtually no affixation or inflection (analytic languages such as Chinese).

In recent decades much greater focus has been given to the lexicon and what information it includes (not only the sound-shapes and meanings of words but information about which words can co-occur with which, which take direct objects – that is, words referring to the object that is acted upon – etc.) as distinct from the morphological component which now links more crucially to syntax. Also, many linguists consider pragmatics, the study of language in units greater than the single sentence, and how language is used in context, to constitute a linguistic level.

In neurology the objects of study of the nineteenth century and part of the twentieth century were the gross areas of brain structure. One primary division was between external surface (cortex) which appeared to have most to do with language, and the larger internal space (subcortical areas) that appeared to have markedly less to do with language. These grosser areas are composed of different cell types and different levels, but as yet we have no knowledge of how individual cells behave specifically in language processing. Nor do we have the neurophysiological knowledge of how electrical messages pulsing down neurons must contribute specifically to language processing in the brain. We will also need to learn how the chemical environment around the cells and their components contributes to language processing; all of these are phenomena that are included in what-we-have-to-learn in neurolinguistics.

Approaches to neurolinguistic study: localizationism and connectionism

Two major schools in the study of neurolinguistics are traditionally described: the localizationists and the holists. In the nineteenth century, localizationists like Broca observed that of the two cerebral hemispheres, one appeared to be responsible for language, the left in most instances. Also, localizationists understood that of all the left hemisphere, the central parts of the outer surface seemed more crucially linked to language, since damage to other parts of the left hemisphere seemed to have very few consequences for language abilities. Then, as different patterns of aphasia were observed, areas within the left-hemisphere cortical language area were parceled out by localizationists, with one area nearer the front of the head deemed responsible for producing language and another, further back, for comprehension, for example.

Speech-language pathologists who have followed a localizationist approach choose to distinguish strongly between patients whose language appears quite fluent on first glance (despite the fact that it is often devoid of meaning) and those who are primarily non-fluent, whose languagee is sparse, slow and effortful, because they know that the brain damage resulting in these two types of aphasia is in markedly different areas of the brain. This localizationist approach has been associated with the "Boston School," after scholars following the teachings of Norman Geschwind, Harold Goodglass and Edith Kaplan at the Aphasia Research Center in Boston. Indeed the behavioral neurologist Geschwind is credited with reading the German neurolinguistic literature of the last century, and bringing its insights to modern-day aphasiological thinking (e.g. Geschwind, 1965).

In recent decades, as we discuss in later chapters (chapters 3, 10, and 12), a technique called cortical stimulation has permitted us to open up the skull and stimulate points on the surface of the brain to glean further knowledge of which areas of the hemispheres are responsible for language processing and which are markedly less involved or not involved at all. More recently positron emission tomography (PET-scans) permits us to observe less invasively how areas of the brain operate. In this sophisticated form of dynamic "x-ray," a picture of the subject's brain can be seen on a computer screen. Different areas of the brain appear to light up while a healthy person is undertaking certain language tasks whereas others light up less or not at all, depending on the amount of activity in a given brain area. Different patterns of activation can be seen for different language tasks, thus encouraging us to think further in terms of localizing language areas responsible for (or to be more cautious, involved heavily in) given linguistic behaviors.

The holist school, by contrast, has argued that localizationism is a false compartmentalizing of language abilities that in fact are supported by larger parts of the brain. Indeed holists were also called "connectionists" (though for reasons we discuss later we avoid that term here) because they focused on how areas of the brain were interconnected. Holists focus more on the ways language is dependent on cognitive abilities such as memory, abstract thinking, attention, etc. and prefer not to limit themselves to exploring ever more delimited language phenomena and language areas. Neurologists such as Hughlings Jackson in the late nineteenth century, and Head and Goldstein earlier in this century were associated with this line of thinking. For Goldstein (1948), for example, "abstract attitude" – our ability to think abstractly – is lost in any sort of brain damage and will necessarily influence language as a result. Speech-language pathologists who follow a holist approach tend not to think in terms of individual syndromes (clusters of symptoms that often occur together) linked to sub-areas of a language area of the brain. They see aphasia as a single phenomenon with patients being more or less severely impaired. Porch and his students have dominated this approach in recent years as did a speech-language pathologist named Hildred Schuell and her colleagues in her 1950s classification of aphasiacs' language problems.

Among the cognitive scientists working in neurolinguistics, it is those who design models of brain processing based on analogies to computer networks, termed the "Parallel Distributed Processing" models, who exemplify a holist approach. Their computer models appear to perform the same functions that language does, and can break down as in the aphasias or learn language with the same

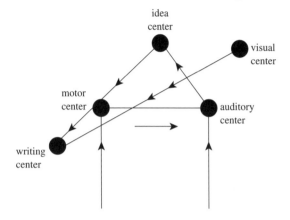

Figure 1.2 Lichtheim's nineteenth-century model for language. (Adapted from Caplan, 1987: 57.)

errors as normals. In the strong form of their theory, there are no language centers per se but rather "network nodes" that are stimulated; eventually one of these is stimulated enough that it passes a certain threshold and that node is "realized," perhaps as a spoken word.

The term "connectionists," amusingly enough, was, in the nineteenth century and early twentieth century, associated with localizationism but is today associated with the holists. The early connectionists were labeled as such because they postulated language centers (such as a center for motor production of speech, another for ideas, another for processing auditory input) and arrows between them that connected them (see Figure 1.2). Today's connectionists, by contrast, are most prototypically proponents of parallel distributed processing. However a new broader label, "interactionists," has been taken on by many in the field and it is sometimes held to be synonymous with "connectionists." Those of us who call ourselves interactionists in the broader sense hold that, while localizing language phenomena in the brain is the eventual goal of neurolinguistics, we no longer expect that there are language areas that are entirely "responsible" for language, or even "dominant" for language, to be contrasted with areas that have nothing to do with it. Rather, indeed, we believe that the whole brain contributes to the broad range of language abilities that neurolinguists should study. We are willing to posit interactions between those areas and processes more crucially contributing to language behaviors and those more crucially contributing to non-language behaviors.

Conclusion

Although the field of neurolinguistics is relatively young, it is an exciting one. Ideas are passionately argued and research in the field is burgeoning. Researchers in the field chip away at the areas they are best trained to work on, joining up with colleagues from others of the related disciplines to shine complementary rays of light on the problems to be solved. In some ways it might seem that we are all waiting for advances in the crucial disciplines: waiting for linguists to settle on the precise best grammar to describe languages, and waiting for neurophysiologists to describe the ways brain cells and their chemical environments contribute to processing it. If we all do our parts in working out how components of those unknown "black boxes" operate, in another decade or three or five, we hope, the contributing disciplines should be able to converge to answer the basic question of neurolinguistics: how the brain is organized for language. In the meantime, neurolinguists get a handle on techniques for extracting knowledge of brain–language relations from patients in whom both are damaged.

Before turning to discussion of methods of studying hemispheric dominance for language and the various pertinent populations of subjects who provide evidence for neurolinguistics, we must consider first, for readers new to the field, how the brain itself is organized.

2 The brain

It is common knowledge that the brain controls muscular activity in the human body. It is clear that the brain is also the seat of conscious thought. Indeed we can all agree that when we have an idea, make the unconscious decision to convey it in language and subsequently actually produce some utterance in our language, the brain is involved at every step along the way. The exact process of the brain's mediation between our thoughts and our linguistic expression of them is still not completely understood, however. In order to understand the knowledge we have acquired and the complexity of the questions that remain unanswered, some basic understanding of the human nervous system is necessary.[1]

Of course, in this introductory book, it is only possible to present a very basic overview of the neuroanatomical structures in the brain. Finer differentiation of cortical and subcortical structures, details about architecture (cellular distribution) and the transmission of neural impulses are the subject matter of more advanced texts (see Suggestions for Further Readings at the end of the book). What is of particular interest to us is the study of interconnections and communication between different structures and regions within and across the brain's hemispheres as well as communication between the brain and the body via the peripheral nervous system (the nerve pathways that lead to and from other body parts).

The human nervous system consists of the central nervous system (the brain and spinal cord) and the peripheral nervous system. The peripheral nervous system includes a system that regulates body functions such as breathing and temperature maintenance. This system is called the autonomic nervous system. Its functions are carried out more or less without our conscious awareness. Although breathing must be coordinated with speech, an understanding of the autonomic nervous system is not necessary for an appreciation of the research described in this book and we will not return to it.

We are, however, concerned with other aspects of the peripheral nervous system. In order to speak, the muscles that control articulators such as the tongue and jaw must be contracted in just the right sequence. If a message is to be written, the muscles in the hand must be properly controlled. For the creation of signs in a visual-gestural language (commonly called a sign language), overall body posture, facial expression and hand movements must all be coordinated. Each of the muscles necessary for communication is controlled by nerves that are connected ultimately to areas in the brain. It will be our goal in this chapter to present information on the components of the central nervous system – and particularly those that contribute to language – and to describe generally its connection to the peripheral nervous system.

Nerves

Each nerve or neuron consists of a cell body and one or more extensions that are similar in function to the electric cords that connect power sources to appliances. These extensions can be extremely long and may carry impulses toward or away from the cell body. The axon of a cell is the extension which carries impulses away from the cell body. Extensions which carry impulses toward the cell body are called dendrites. For example, a motor neuron located in the spinal cord may have an axon which extends all of the way through the legs and ends in the muscle fibers of the toes. A schematic drawing of a generic motor neuron is seen in Figure 2.1. The reader is left to imagine the possibility of an axon extending several feet rather than inches.

One single axon may control the movement of a number of muscle fibers. The nerve cell body, its axon and the muscle fibers it controls are called a motor unit. Different muscles have different

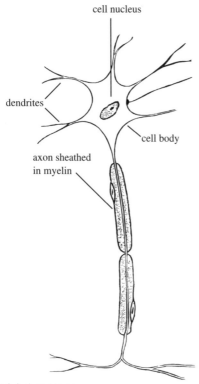

Figure 2.1 A motor neuron.

numbers of muscle fibers. The number of muscle fibers controlled by a nerve cell is also not the same for all muscles. A particular muscle may have a number of muscle fibers per motor unit ranging from under 100 to 2,000. If a muscle, such as the muscle of the thigh, has a very large number of muscle fibers per motor unit, that muscle, being controlled by only a small number of nerves, will not be capable of delicate movements. If, on the other hand, many nerves control the movement of separate muscle fibers in a muscle, as in the mouth, a more precise degree of control can be exercised.

A motor neuron exercises control of the muscle fibers in its motor unit by causing the electrochemical changes necessary to force the contraction of the muscle. This is possible because each muscle fiber in the unit has the motor ending from a peripheral nerve (see Figure 2.2). When a nerve impulse reaches these motor endings, a substance called acetylcholine is released. This substance combines with a receptor substance and makes the changes necessary to the muscle cell membrane in order to cause contraction of the muscle.

The simplified description above brings the reader only from the spinal cord to the skeletal muscle. We must also understand the origination of nerve impulses in the brain as well as pathways that lead from sensory receptors to the brain. It is also important to realize that while flexing one's toes is fairly readily understood using the above description, much more subtle issues of timing arise when considering complex movements such as talking. For example, the tongue is controlled by a cranial nerve pair called the hypoglossal nerves. Each hypoglossal nerve goes to one half of the tongue. Complex messages from the brain must be sent in order to control the tongue properly for speech. For example, the difference between the [t] and [k] sounds in English cannot be described in terms of simple contraction or relaxation of "the tongue." The entire shape of the tongue is different for these two sounds. For [t], the tip of the tongue touches the front part of the roof of the mouth. For [k] it is the back of the tongue that touches the back of the roof of the mouth. This will become particularly important in our discussion of speech planning and speech errors in the chapters on aphasia, chapters 4 and 5.

The central nervous system

The spinal cord itself – that bundle of nerves connecting the brain and peripheral body parts – is housed within the spinal column. The spinal column is a series of individual bones or vertebrae each of which has a hollow center and openings at the sides. The bones are joined together by cartilage to form a column which begins at the base of the skull, extends the length of the back, and ends in the coccyx or "tail-bone." Its purpose is to support the body, allow movement of the torso and protect the spinal cord, which, along with protective fluids, fills the hollow

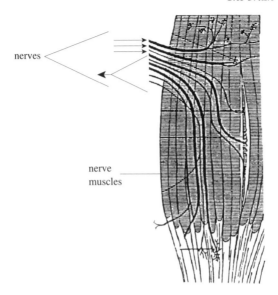

Figure 2.2 A schematic of motor neurons controlling muscle fibers. (Adapted from Gardner, 1968: 147.)

centers of the column. The side openings in the vertebrae allow for pairs of spinal nerves to go out from and into the spinal cord.

The spinal cord actually continues up into the skull where it is joined with the brain stem, sometimes called the "primitive brain" because it is involved with maintaining unconscious functions such as consciousness and breathing. Wedged between the brain stem and the back of the cerebrum (discussed below) is the cerebellum. The cerebellum is comprised of two hemispheres joined by a middle piece. It is an important structure for the control of muscles.

The brain hemispheres

Although a cursory knowledge of all of the structures of the central nervous system provides context for a full understanding of research concerning brain representation for language, the largest portion of the human brain, and by far the most important for issues in speech and language is the cerebrum. Some basic facts about the cerebrum are obvious from an initial observation. (See Figure 2.3.) The cerebrum, like the cerebellum, is divided into two hemispheres, right and left. The cerebral hemispheres are not entirely separate; they are connected by fiber bundles, the most important of which is the corpus callosum. The surface of the cerebral hemispheres is the cortex which is distinguished by its convolutions: the hills and valleys known as *gyri* and *sulci* respectively. These can be seen in Figures 2.3 and 2.4.

A closer look at each hemisphere shows that certain of the gyri and sulci are particularly pronounced and can be used to delimit four lobes; the temporal, occipital, parietal and frontal lobes. The important sulci, gyri, and lobes are marked in Figure 2.4. The Rolandic fissure separates the frontal and parietal lobes; the Sylvian fissure cuts through the language area, with the temporal lobe below and the parietal and frontal lobes above. The frontal lobe is often referred to as an *anterior* region of the brain; the parietal lobe is *posterior* to it, as is the occipital lobe. As the temporal lobe runs from front to back, it has both anterior and posterior sections.

Another approach to delimiting regions within the cerebral hemispheres is to study the types of cells to be found in each region, as a neuropathologist, Korbinian Brodmann, did last century. The subtle differences in density of cell types are represented schematically in Figure 2.5. The upper picture represents the visible surface of a hemisphere. The lower picture represents the part that faces the other hemisphere.

The outer surface or cortex of both cerebral hemispheres is grayish in appearance if the brain is dissected and stained after death. This outer layer consists mostly of nerve cell bodies and is referred to as "gray matter." Beneath the gray matter are the sub-cortical regions or "white matter" which consists for the most part of nerve cell fibers. There are, however, additional areas of "gray matter" on the insides of the cerebral hemispheres. Figure 2.6 shows a slice of the brain prepared with a stain which colors only gray matter.

Although the cortex is most crucial for language, subcortical areas also participate. Most of the subcortical areas are seen as white matter when staining techniques are used. Some specific

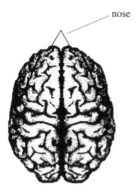

Figure 2.3 Looking down on the two cortical hemispheres. (Adapted from Sidman and Sidman, 1965: 193.)

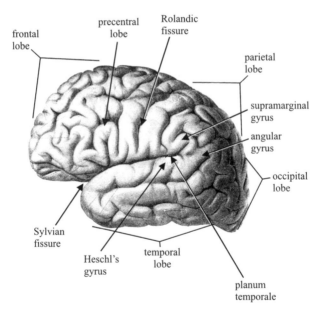

Figure 2.4 Important lobes, fissures, and gyri of the cortex.

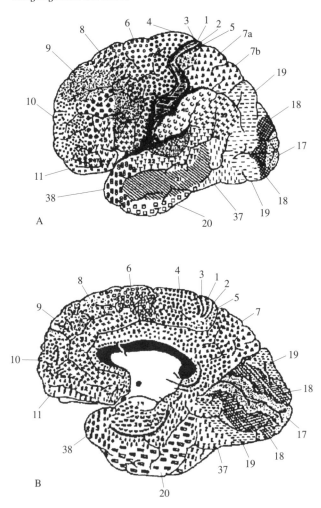

Figure 2.5 Brodmann's map of different cell types in (A) the outer surface of the cortex and (B) the surface that faces the other hemisphere. (Adapted from Spreen et al., 1984: 7 and Strong, 1959: 449.)

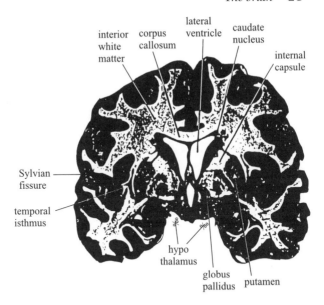

Figure 2.6 Subcortical areas of interest. Picture of a brain sliced parallel to the face. Above the Sylvian fissure we see the frontal lobe; below it the temporal lobe. The staining technique renders the gray matter black and the white matter unstained. (Adapted from Gardner, 1968: 21.)

structures in the center of the brain are gray matter, however, such as the thalamus and hypothalamus. These structures are primarily involved with more basic functions than language (e.g. sleep, appetite, sexual desire). However, one ridge of white matter among them, the internal capsule, is implicated in aphasia. Also the temporal isthmus along with the arcuate fasciculus connects anterior and posterior cortical areas involved in language.

Individual differences in development of the brain

The many structures described above all originate from the neural plate, a single layer of cells which develops in the middle of the back of human embryos early in gestation. This single layer begins to differentiate into three layers of distinct cell types. The amazing neuroanatomical complexity of the brain is realized through a continued differentiation of cell types and migration of cells to distinct locations in the developing brain. Each stage is dependent on both genetic messages and fetal hormonal environment.

It has been suggested (Geschwind & Behan, 1982, Geschwind & Galaburda, 1985) that the presence of some unusual traits in individuals and individual families may be attributed to an unusual fetal hormonal environment. A certain balance of hormones helps trigger normal fetal development. In these individuals, they posit, unusual amounts of certain hormones – especially testosterone – at crucial stages around the third and fourth months of fetal development – trigger unusual patterns of brain development. The basic tenets of the "Geschwind/Galaburda Hypothesis" can be summarized as follows:

> During the third and fourth months of fetal growth, three systems are developing: the system for lateral dominance whereby one hemisphere of the brain will be responsible for handedness and language, the endocrinological system, and the immune system. Unusual hormonal events, that tend to run in families, they hypothesize, may lead to cells migrating in unusual patterns. This may result in underdevelopment in certain areas (say those necessary for reading in the dyslexic child who will have difficulty learning to read) and overdevelopment of other areas – either contiguous ones in the same hemisphere, or analogous ones in the other hemisphere. This overdevelopment may be responsible for special talents (such as music or math) as well as disabilities. Whatever causes this unusual hemispheric development appears to result in unusual immune system phenomena (e.g. a proneness to allergies) as well as unusual endocrinological phenomena (e.g. twinning and, in their analysis, homosexuality).

The possibility of subtle individual differences in brain organization adds another dimension of complexity to the study of brain representation for language. We will return to these issues in the sections in later chapters on language performance in left-handers and talented second language acquisition.

Cortical brain regions important for language

In this section we must consider the lobes and subsections in greater detail than we did earlier in this chapter. Although both afferent (toward the brain) and efferent (away from the brain) fibers are present in most parts of the cerebral cortex, some regions have a particularly high concentration of fibers of one or another type. For example, there is an area (Brodmann's area 4, see Figure 2.5) that lies at the back of the frontal lobe just in front of the Rolandic fissure, that contains mostly fibers that lead to motor neurons, those responsible for generating movement. By electrically stimulating the cells in this area, it has been possible to "map out" the motor cortex, that is to determine where nerve impulses that control the musculature in various areas must originate. An example of such a generally agreed upon map of the motor cortex is found below (see Figure 2.7).

This primary motor area, or motor strip, exists in both hemispheres of the cerebral cortex. Stimulating a cortical area in one hemisphere usually makes the muscles on the opposite side of the body move. This is because most of the nerve fibers cross over to the opposite or contralateral side. There is some representation in each cerebral hemisphere for the ipsilateral or same-side muscles but the strongest connections are those that run to the opposite side.

Similarly, it has been possible to determine which cortical areas contain nerve fibers that receive sensory input, the somatosensory areas. The various areas of the body send sensory information to a cortical area in the contralateral hemisphere area just across the Rolandic fissure from the motor strip. This primary somatosensory area is in the front of the parietal lobe.

The primary area for the reception of visual stimuli is in the occipital lobe. The representation of visual information is somewhat more complex than the brain representation for muscles. In the motor cortex, it is possible to say more or less accurately that the motor cortex of the left hemisphere controls movement of the right side of the body. Most of the visual pathways are also contralateral. However, rather than information from the right *eye* coming to the left hemisphere, information from the *right visual field* comes to the left hemisphere. The visual field is the area which can be seen without movement of the head or eyes. The midpoint in that field is the dividing line between the left and right visual fields. Both eyes see both fields. Both the left and right eye send information about the left visual field to the right hemisphere and

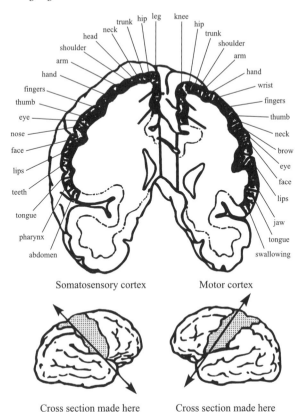

Figure 2.7 Motor and sensory cortex. (Adapted from Donner, "Brain function and blood flow," in *Scientific American*, 1978: 64 and 68.)

information about the right visual field to the left hemisphere (see Figure 2.8). Of course, information can be shared between the two hemispheres because they are connected by the corpus callosum (see Figure 2.8).

The temporal lobe contains Heschl's gyrus, a structure particularly important for the reception of auditory stimuli. Again, there are both contralateral and ipsilateral pathways between the ears and the cerebral hemispheres, but the contralateral pathways are the predominant ones.

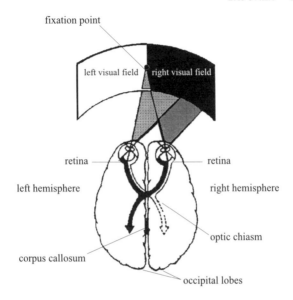

Figure 2.8 Visual pathways. (Adapted from Schneider and Tarshish, *An Intro-duction to Physiological Psychology*, McGraw Hill, 3rd edn, 1986: 645.)

If one pulls the temporal lobe away from the parietal lobe, over Heschl's gyrus and extending to the juncture between the tem-poral and parietal lobes lies the *planum temporale*. Because this area of cortex is markedly larger in the left hemisphere of most humans than in the right, and because it is contiguous to the other lan-guage areas, it is considered important for language (see Figure 2.4) as a secondary association area.

Indeed, contiguous to each of the primary areas (namely the motor strip for outgoing speech and Heschl's gyrus for perceiving speech) are secondary association areas where a higher level of processing takes place. Behind Heschl's gyrus is Wernicke's area (discussed in chapter 4) which appears to be necessary for making sense out of the auditory stimuli that come in and are judged by the primary auditory area to be speech, rather than non-language noises. In front of the primary motor area is Broca's area (also discussed in chapter 4) which is involved in motor planning (and perhaps syntactic processing) specific for speech.

Behind Wernicke's area lies the inferior parietal lobule. It is composed of two gyri: the supramarginal gyrus, and, behind that, the angular gyrus. These are considered to be a tertiary association area, connecting the secondary association areas for auditory, visual, and somasthetic processing. This area is also called the temporo-parieto-occipital junction as these three lobes meet here.

Conclusion

Nerve cells both in the cortical surface and in subcortical areas of the brain hemispheres are involved in both producing and understanding language. Within the left hemisphere, a "language area" can be delimited that includes areas right next to the primary motor areas of the brain and the primary sensory areas, as well as areas further back involved in taking in information presented either visually or auditorially.

3 How we know what we know about brain organization for language

Left-hemisphere dominance for language

The search for localized brain centers for speech and language has a long and interesting history. The first group of neurologists to search for an area of the brain dedicated to language function were the phrenologists of the early nineteenth century to whom we referred earlier. Proponents of this school of thought believed that particular talents or personality traits manifested themselves in increased development in particular cortical areas with subsequent effects on the actual shape of the cranium or skull. Close examination of the skull, they believed, could lead to an understanding of the inner person. The phrenologists, such as Gall in England, Spurzheim in Germany and Bouillaud in France, believed the language faculty to be located in the two frontal lobes. In fact Bouillaud went as far as to offer a prize to anyone who could find a patient with linguistic deficits and no frontal lobe damage! There was some disagreement among phrenologists as to whether there was a single language faculty or perhaps, as Gall suggested, one center for the memory of words and another for articulate speech (Brown & Chobor, 1992).

Data from brain damage

As early as 1836, John Abercrombie, a prominent Scottish physician, published data from which the association of left-brain damage with linguistic deficits was clear. As Hans Forstl (1991) points out in his review of Abercrombie's work, it was probably a reaction to the rather fanciful drawing of conclusions in phrenology that led Abercrombie to publish his observations without drawing attention to the obvious conclusion of left-hemisphere dominance for language.

More often cited as the first linking of the left hemisphere to language is the 1836 paper of Marc Dax, "Lesions of the Left Half of the Brain Associated with the Loss of Signs of Thought," which represented the results of Dax's study on a large series of brain-injured patients. Forstl (1991) attributes the fact that this significant work was never published to the strength of the phrenological camp.

In fact it is the neurologist/anthropologist Paul Broca who is credited with discovering, and reporting in his 1865 paper, that language loss after brain injury was far more common after left-sided injury than after right-sided injury. More recent studies suggest that approximately 97% of the population has language represented predominantly in the left hemisphere. Of the remaining 3%, most are left-handed. Since we estimate that some 10% of the population is left-handed, this means that the majority of left-handed individuals also have language represented in their left hemisphere.

How do we know that 3% of the population has language represented primarily in the right hemisphere? There are a certain number of cases of "crossed aphasia"; that is right-handers with language deficits after right-sided injury. It was evident even in the series examined by Abercrombie in the 1800s that there was a small percentage of people with right-hemisphere representation for language.

Data from anesthetizing one hemisphere

In more recent times we have also been able to determine the dominant hemisphere for language in uninjured brains. In a technique called the Wada test, an anesthetic called sodium amytal is injected into the artery leading to one side of the brain or the other. If the drug is delivered to the language side of the brain, a temporary paralysis of language function is experienced. The patient stands with both arms extended forward from the shoulders. Slowly the arm opposite the patient's "language" hemisphere – usually the right arm – goes down as the brain areas of that opposite hemisphere that should be available for keeping it up are no longer operating. The patient cannot speak at all for several minutes and in the minutes after that, language sounds aphasic, somewhat like the first patient cited at the beginning of the first chapter.

The results of this test confirm the statistics from incidence of aphasia after brain injury. Among right-handers with no history of early left-brain damage, approximately 95% experience temporary interference with language after an injection of sodium amytal into the left carotid artery, which brings blood to the left hemisphere. Approximately 70% of left-handers experience similar interference after left carotid injection. Of the remaining 30%, half only have temporary paralysis of language function after right carotid injection. The other half would seem to have at least some degree of bilateral speech control (Hécaen & Albert, 1978). The numbers for manual/visual languages may be a bit different. Some signers exhibit aphasic symptoms after left hemisphere injection of sodium-amytal (Damasia et al., 1986). However, there is some research suggesting greater right hemisphere involvement in processing sign language (see Poizner, Klima & Bellugi, 1987, for a review). The Wada test is used primarily as a method of determining which hemisphere is dominant for language in patients who must undergo brain surgery. The brains of these surgery patients, frequently epileptics for whom medications have not worked to control the epilepsy, while not acutely injured, by definition have some neurological problem. In neurologically normal populations, there would likely be even less indication of bilateral representation for speech/language.

Tachistoscopic presentation

It is also possible to present visual stimuli selectively to one hemisphere or the other in normal individuals in order to learn about which hemisphere is involved in processing them. When a person looks at a point, everything to the right of that point is in the right visual field. Everything to the left of that point is in the left visual field. Ordinarily, both eyes see both visual fields. However, information about the right visual field is sent by both eyes to the left hemisphere and information about the left visual field is sent by both eyes to the right hemisphere. Recall that Figure 2.8 illustrates the normal operation of visual perception.

The technique called tachistoscopic presentation allows normal subjects to react to a visual stimulus presented to only one visual field. The stimulus is flashed to one or the other side of the fixation point so briefly that the subjects do not have time to change their gaze, allowing the image to be part of the other visual field. In normal subjects the left and right visual areas of the brain communicate via the corpus callosum. This means that information will be processed regardless of the visual field in which it is presented. However, linguistic stimuli will be processed more quickly and more accurately when presented to the right visual field (left hemisphere). Such a pattern can be seen in tachistoscopic testing over a number of stimuli. While tachistoscopic presentation is not as accurate as brain damage in indicating which side of the brain is dominant for language (only between 60% and 70% of normals demonstrate a left-hemisphere dominance for language, for example, via tachistoscopic presentation, while from brain damage studies we know the numbers should be higher, closer to 97%), the technique is certainly non-invasive, and thus substantial numbers of tachistoscopic studies have been conducted since the 1950s to determine which hemisphere is dominant for different aspects of language and non-language processing.

The dichotic listening technique

A second technique that has been developed to study lateral dominance in normal individuals is called *dichotic listening*. While tachistoscopic presentation uses visual stimuli, dichotic presentation uses auditory stimuli. This technique relies on the fact that the right ear has stronger connections to the left hemisphere than it does to the right (and conversely for the left ear). Thus information presented to the right ear, while it will be sent to both hemispheres' auditory centers, will be better processed contralaterally. Under normal circumstances, we see no effects of this curious organization, but when we "overload the system," we can infer that one hemisphere or the other performs better for a given sort of stimulus type. For example, if normal subjects hear triads of different words presented simultaneously to both ears (the right ear might hear "2," "8," "5" while the left ear hears "9," "1," "6"), and asked to repeat back everything they hear, most subjects are more likely to forget "1," the information that went to the left ear – that is, the right hemisphere – from the mid-point of the triad. Over a number of trials, we can see a consistent performance for language materials like these numbers that is the opposite of the pattern we see for non-verbal meaningful materials such as babies' cries, fire sirens, bird whistles, etc. This technique, then, complements tachistoscopic presentation in allowing us to evaluate lateral dominance for spoken language as well as written language. As with tachistoscopic presentation, it does not give us the same clarity that explicit brain damage does, but it is infinitely easier to manipulate.

Split-brain patients

Under normal circumstances, the two halves of the brain work in tandem. Sensory information travels along pathways from one side of the body to the opposite side of the brain. Acoustic stimuli arrive at the brain along both contralateral and ipsilateral pathways. Visual information from each visual hemifield is sent to the opposite hemisphere (see Figure 2.8). In the normal human brain, all of this information is shared between the two hemispheres as signals are passed via the corpus callosum, the bundle of some 200 million nerve fibers connecting the left and right hemispheres. There is, however, a small but well-studied population of individuals in whom this inter-hemispheric communication is no longer possible. The same fibers which allow for the sharing of information between the two hemispheres unfortunately also allow for the electrical misfirings which result in a kind of intractable, epileptic seizure. In some cases the only way to allow the patient to live productively is to sever the main inter-hemispheric connections in a process called a commissurotomy. This procedure was developed in the 1940s and 1950s but its use declined as better drugs were developed for managing epilepsy. The everyday behavior of these "split-brain" patients is essentially normal. Occasional eerie reports of dissociation of behavior of the left and right sides of the body are reported. Some patients report difficulty in learning new name-face connections. The right hemisphere seems to be particularly involved in interpreting visuo-spatial information, in this case, the appearance of the new face. The left hemisphere will process the new linguistic information: the name. It is not surprising that this particular kind of learning would be problematic after a commissurotomy. Beginning in the 1950s, many experiments were performed testing the linguistic abilities of the isolated left and right hemispheres in these patients.

One type of experiment has the split-brain patient sit at a table with a screen blocking the view of objects on the other side. If the patient reaches behind the screen with the left hand, tactile information about the object is conveyed only to the right hemisphere and the person will be unable to name the object held. Objects not seen, but held in the right hand are readily named. The isolated right hemisphere can process the tactile information. It can guide the left hand to choose a similar item from an array of items, but it cannot name the item. From such a study we can learn what language the isolated right hemisphere can process and how independent the isolated left hemisphere can be in processing language (see chapter 7).

Localization of language within the left hemisphere

The dominance of the left hemisphere for language for most people is largely uncontroversial. Determining the particular left hemisphere areas involved in the various aspects of language comprehension and production is more difficult.

History

The claim that linguistic ability is localized in a particular area of the left hemisphere is generally credited to the French neurologist Paul Broca. In 1861 (interestingly, four years before he noted that left- but not right-sided brain damage seemed to result in language disturbance) he presented data that implicated the area of the frontal lobe just in front of the Sylvian fissure in language function. In 1874, Carl Wernicke demonstrated that for two patients he had seen, damage to an area in back of the Sylvian fissure had caused linguistic deficits. The trends toward describing very specific left-hemisphere areas and ascribing specific language functions to these areas continued for some time. Henderson et al. (1992) quote a prominent professor of medicine, Ludwig Lichtheim, who wrote that once aphasiologists had determined the ways in which language functions were localized and interconnected in the brain, neurologists "should then be able to determine the exact place of any discontinuity in these paths and account for its symptomatic manifestations with the same precision as we do for those of a motor or sensory paralysis depending on a lesion of the peripheral nerves" (Lichtheim, 1885).

As Henderson explains, not all neurologists of the late nineteenth century were comfortable with this narrow delimitation of speech centers. Hughlings Jackson (1878) pointed out that "to locate the damage which destroys speech and to locate speech are two different things." Freud (1891) agreed with Jackson's skepticism in interpreting aphasiological data. For Freud, it seemed likely that there was only one type of aphasia. Different symptoms such as those found in Broca's vs. Wernicke's patients (discussed in the next two chapters) were to be explained by the proximity of the patients' lesions to either motor or sensory areas in the left hemisphere.

Modern aphasiologists are still not entirely in agreement over the extent to which specific language functions are subserved by specific brain areas. The details of some of these debates will be the material for the following chapters. However, even the "localizationists" of today have heeded the cautions of the past, as can be seen from a comparison of Lichtheim's schematic drawing of brain representation for language (Figure 1.2) and a modern schematic drawing of the language areas of the left hemisphere (Figure 1.1).

Cortical stimulation

One modern technique that is useful in determining which areas of the left hemisphere are involved in language processing is called *cortical stimulation.* Consider the maps one can make of left-hemisphere sites where electrical stimulation interferes with naming ability in hearing individuals.

In order to determine which cortical areas of the brain are involved in speech production in patients who need to have brain tissue removed because of intractable epilepsy, electrical stimulation of the brain surface is used to make a map of the patient's brain. The brain does not contain pain receptors so patients may remain conscious and attempt to name pictured items while electrical stimulation is being applied to different points in their brains (See Figure 3.1). If the stimulation is in an area of the brain normally involved in speech, it interferes with patients' ability to name; they may be totally unable to speak or unable only to name a simple picture of an object. Alternately, they may experience hesitation, slurring or repetition in attempts at naming the pictured object. This interference *never* follows the stimulation of parts of the non-language-dominant half of the patient's brain (Penfield & Roberts, 1959).

It is of interest to consider the effects of cortical stimulation on a signed language. Haglund et al., 1993, tested a woman who had learned American Sign Language (ASL) as a child. Left-hemisphere stimulation affected both languages but some areas affected primarily ASL and other areas affected primarily English.

Imaging techniques

Only recently have imaging techniques such as CAT-scans (Computerized Axial Tomography), PET-scans (Positron Emission Tomography) and MRIs (Magnetic Resonance Imaging) offered precise information about lesion sites in living patients.

In these techniques, people's brains are "x-rayed" and computer programs convert the pictures into maps we can recognize. CT-scans are good at localizing many sorts of lesions, but not very recent ones or ones very close to the skull. MRI scans can demon-

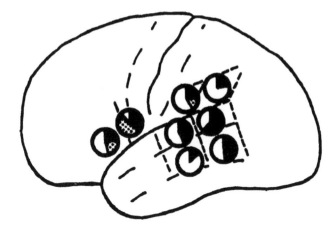

Figure 3.1 A cortical stimulation map. Filled areas of circles indicate the percentage of patients with anomia when stimulation is at that point. (Adapted from G. Ojemann, Brain organization for language from the perspective of electrical stimulation mapping, *Behavioral and Brain Science*, 1983, 6: 199.)

strate some of the lesions that CAT-scans cannot. PET-scans can provide ongoing pictures of the changes in brain activation over time (e.g. glucose uptake that occurs when an area of the brain needs oxygen for more strenuous activity), and thus could provide the best evidence of how language processing takes place dynamically. However the pictures PET-scans provide are much fuzzier than those of MRIs.

Currently many new imaging techniques are competing to provide crisp pictures of brain activities as they take place. One such solution is the evoked potential technique. This is used with normal subjects by attaching a number of electrodes on the scalp and then seeing which ones show electrical activity in the brain milliseconds after some stimulus has involved one or more areas of the brain that have thus emitted an electrical response. This technique is often abbreviated as ERP, standing for "event-related evoked potential." The "event" is the stimulus; the evoked potential is the electrical response in the brain that can be read through the scalp.

A second imaging technique of interest is the fMRI, "functional

MRIs;" like cartoons they provide a series of snapshots of brain activity so quickly that we appear to see a continuous process unfold on the video screen. (See chapter 12 for more information on these imaging techniques.)

Conclusion

Even armed with precise information about lesion sites, we cannot escape the difficulty inherent in studying brain damage. Individual brain representation for language may vary. Lesions cannot be expected to damage only areas that functioned together before the brain damage. Also, investigators' views on normal language influence the structure of the tasks administered to their patients. Yet, in spite of these many difficulties, substantial progress has been made in creating a map of a general language area in the brain. Converging evidence from studies of aphasia, sodium amytal injection, split-brain patients, and tachistoscopic and dichotic presentation points to left-hemisphere dominance for language organization and processing in most humans (but see chapter 7 for right-hemisphere contributions). Aphasia lesions, cortical stimulation, and the brain-imaging techniques permit us to delimit a "language area" within the left hemisphere around the Sylvian fissure.

4 Aphasia: classification of the syndromes

Introduction

The human brain is well protected by the skull. Yet there are a number of possible ways for the brain to become injured. During a collision, the brain can be smashed against the skull with enough force to create a "closed head injury." Something (a bullet, knife, piece of metal, etc.) might strike the skull with enough force to penetrate it. Or the problem could originate inside the skull, with infection, tumor, or broken blood vessels damaging brain tissue. No matter what the cause of the brain injury, it is unlikely that the entire brain will be equally affected. Some areas will be "harder hit" than others.

When the brain is injured, the problems of the patient will vary depending on the extent and location of the damage. A particular injury might cause only visual problems or problems only in moving certain sets of muscles. The injuries of particular interest to us in this chapter are those that cause problems with language. In our efforts to understand the brain representation for language, we will need to look carefully to see which locations in the brain will lead to language problems after injury and which locations will not. As noted earlier, language deficits acquired after brain injury are called "aphasia." We will see that not all "aphasics," that is, people with aphasia, have the same symptoms.

The most devastating kind of linguistic deficit is the total inability to communicate using language. The patient cannot speak more than a few words or syllables, and understands very little. When this type of deficit persists, it is referred to as "global aphasia" and is usually the consequence of damage to large portions of the left hemisphere of the brain. However, not all patients who are completely unable to communicate immediately following a brain injury are true global aphasics. In some cases, the patient's condition resolves over weeks or months into partial deficits. In rare instances, there can also be complete recovery. In patients who do experience complete recovery of their linguistic abilities after being totally aphasic in the time immediately after their injury, we see evidence that linguistic competence – their inner knowledge of language – may be preserved even in cases of severe problems with "performance," that is, impairment in speaking or understanding language. The only alternative explanation would be that the patients somehow reconstructed their grammar in the relatively brief time between injury and recovery.

Patients with less extensive damage will, as a rule, have less extensive loss of linguistic abilities. To the extent that different sets of symptoms are associated with injuries in different brain areas, we can develop a more detailed map of language functions in the brain. In aphasia, we see language difficulties without cognitive impairment. Such patients may produce only sparse and disconnected words, but have no trouble on non-verbal tests of IQ, nor trouble cooking, or walking a complex route home. Other brain-damaged patients may, by contrast, exhibit cognitive impairment without linguistic difficulties. These patients produce and comprehend language well, but show problems on tests of memory for visually presented non-verbal material, puzzle completion, and other non-verbal IQ tests. Such problems affect daily tasks such as cooking, memory for common routes, and the like. In light of the linguists' concept of a mental grammar made up of various sub-components (phonology, syntax etc.), we might expect language breakdown to occur along exactly these lines. One patient might have trouble with sentence formulation and another with word formation or pronunciation. We might also expect processing problems to be different from production problems. And in fact we believe that the differential sparing of phonological, morphological, syntactic, and semantic abilities in aphasic patients speaks grossly for the organization of linguistic components as described by linguists (see chapter 11). However, when we look at the actual language produced by people with brain injuries and at their comprehension abilities, we begin to see that the correspondence between symptoms and site of injury, and between linguists' grammars and patients' deficits is not nearly as simple as it might be.

In the remaining pages of this chapter we will present some general facts about syndromes – common clusters of symptoms – seen in aphasia in monolingual adults, and the brain areas they are associated with (see summary Table 4.1). This chapter will provide the background necessary for an appreciation of the more detailed studies presented in the next chapter. In that chapter we will treat specific symptoms like agrammatism and look at some interesting controversies, where the language produced by a group of aphasics could be explained by more than one possible understanding of language organization.

Broca's aphasia

In his famous 1861 paper the French neurologist, Broca, presented data from a patient called "Tan" or "Tan Tan" in the literature, as "Tan" was the only syllable he could speak. Tan repeated "Tan" as necessary, with good intonation, as if to convey a message. His comprehension was relatively spared, and he appeared irritated he could not get his message across. A postmortem examination of his brain showed the lesion – the area of brain damage – to be confined mostly to the lower areas of the left frontal lobe. This area became known as Broca's area (see Figure 1.1). Great difficulties with producing speech became known as Broca's aphasia, although more characteristic than the extremely severe aphasia of Tan Tan is a somewhat milder form. The classic Broca's aphasic in today's taxonomy is considered "non-fluent" in that his speech is slow, deliberate, and effortful, often with omission of grammatical markers (e.g. "Boy go store" instead of "The boy has gone to the store"). Yet comprehension is spared.

Consider the following speech sample from a Broca's aphasic. The patient, L.M., was a sixty-four-year-old man who had a stroke which damaged a large portion of his left hemisphere, leaving him paralyzed on his right side. He also experienced a number of language problems including some problems with naming and

Table 4.1. *Aphasia symptoms*

Syndrome	Speech	Comprehension	Repetition	Naming	Lesion site[a]
Broca's aphasia	poor, non-fluent	good	poor	poor	anterior
Wernicke's aphasia	fluent, empty	poor	poor	poor	posterior
Conduction aphasia	fluent	good	poor	poor	arcuate fasciculus
Anomic aphasia	fluent with circumlocutions	good	good	poor	anywhere
Global aphasia	virtually none	poor	poor	poor	large
Transcortical motor aphasia	little	good	good	not bad	outside in frontal lobe
Transcortical sensory aphasia	fluent	poor	good	poor	outside in parietal lobe

Note: [a]*Lesion site* refers to areas in or relative to the language zone delimited in Figure 1.1. Thus "anterior" means "the anterior part of the language area;" "anywhere" means "anywhere in the language area."

repetition. He was able to understand everyday conversations but did not do well on tests of comprehension of complex syntax. His most marked difficulty was in the production of speech. As part of his evaluation he was asked to describe the picture below which is known as the "cookie theft picture" from the Boston diagnostic aphasia examination (Goodglass and Kaplan, 1972). (See Figure 4.1) His description follows (the examiner's remarks are in square brackets):

> kid . . . kk . . can . . . candy . . . cookie . . . caandy . . . well I don't know but it's writ . . . easy does it . . . slam . . . early . . . fall . . . men . . . many no . . . girl. dishes . . . soap . . . soap . . . water . . . water . . . falling pah that's all . . . dish . . . that's all.
>
> cookies . . . can . . . candy . . . cookies   cookies . . . he . . . down . . . That's all. Girl . . . slipping water . . . water . . . and it hurts . . . much to do . .Her . . . clean up . . . Dishes . . . up there . . . I think that's doing it [The examiner asks: What is she doing with the dishes?] discharge no . . . I forgot . . . dirtying clothes [?] dish [?] water . . . [The examiner probes: What about it?] slippery water . . . [?] scolded . . . slipped

In this brief excerpt of the patient's speech we can see some of the common features of the speech of non-fluent aphasics. His speech is effortful with pauses, false starts, and unclear words. He seems to have some word-finding difficulty ("discharge" for 'washing dishes') and he seems to be aware of his difficulties ("no . . . I forgot"). Only a few stock phrases are repeated smoothly ("easy does it" and "that's all," for example). Nouns are the most common words in this excerpt, however verbs also occur relatively frequently. Functors (that is, articles, prepositions and other free grammatical morphemes) as well as bound morphemes (that is inflectional and derivational affixes) are rare.

Wernicke's aphasia

In 1874 the German neurologist Carl Wernicke presented information on two patients whose speech was markedly different from that of Broca's patient. Their speech was relatively "fluent" – that is, the intonation and pace appeared normal – but it contained unusual semantic features. The patients would frequently use elaborate descriptions, called "circumlocutions," instead of

Figure 4.1 The Cookie Theft picture of the Boston Diagnostic Aphasia Examination. (Reprinted from Goodglass and Kaplan, 1983.)

simple words. Sometimes words would be only barely recognizable because of phonemic substitutions. At other times the patients would create new words altogether; these came to be called "neologisms." Unlike Broca's patient, Tan Tan, whose comprehension seemed unimpaired, the comprehension of these patients was severely impaired. Their lesions were posterior to the lesion Broca had identified in Tan Tan; in Wernicke's patients the damage was in the area at the back and top of the temporal lobe now known as Wernicke's area. The collection of symptoms he described is now known as Wernicke's aphasia, and it is characteristic of damage to Wernicke's area (see Figure 1.1).

The following sample from the speech of A.M., a seventy-five-year-old man with Wernicke's aphasia, presents a striking contrast to the speech of the Broca's aphasic, L.M. Although pauses and word-finding problems are also found, A.M.'s speech flows much more freely. Grammatical morphemes occur quite frequently, although overall sentence structure can be somewhat bizarre.

An excerpt from an interview with him follows. A.M. has been asked what brought him to the hospital. The examiner's interpretations are in square brackets:

> Is this some of the work that we work as we did before? ... All right ... From when wine [why] I'm here. What's wrong with me because I ... was myself until the taenz took something about the time between me and my regular time in that time and they took the time in that time here and that's when the the time took around here and saw me around in it it's started with me no time and then I bekan [began] work of nothing else that's the way the doctor find me that way ....

Two problems apparent in the speech of A.M., which we did not find in the speech of the non-fluent aphasic, are misselections of the sounds of words (called phonemic paraphasias – e.g. "wine" for "why") and a lack of meaningful content. Although one can find phonemic paraphasias in Broca's aphasics, they occur with far less frequency. The characteristic "off" syntax (e.g. "What's wrong with me because ...") is called paragrammatism.

Conduction aphasia

The most widely discussed other aphasic syndrome is "conduction aphasia." The key symptom of conduction aphasia is an inability to repeat spoken language. It was originally conceived of as a disconnection of Broca's and Wernicke's areas due to damage to the structure that connects them known as the arcuate fasciculus (see Figure 1.1).

In conduction aphasics, a relatively spared Broca's area was thought to control the motor functions necessary for producing spontaneous speech, and a relatively spared Wernicke's area was thought to allow for good comprehension. Repetition, however, requires rapid communication between the two areas via the arcuate fasciculus according to this model, so the patients' ability to repeat was impaired. Since it is unusual to find a lesion restricted exactly to this area, patients might have some comprehension and/or production difficulty as well, but their repetition would be markedly more impaired. In the next chapter we discuss the more current understanding of conduction aphasia.

Anomic aphasia

All patients with aphasia of any type have anomia, that is, problems remembering the names of things, but one set of relatively mildly impaired patients are called "anomic aphasics" because their naming problem is their only language problem. Asked to name the picture of a pen, for example, an anomic patient might say "Oh, right, one of those things you use for writing – not, a pencil – I have one right here." The cognitive psychologist Ashcraft (1993) wrote about a temporary anomia he experienced as the result of an aneurysm – a ballooning of one of his brain's arteries that drew blood away from his language area. One day Ashcraft was sitting at his desk when his assistant came in to ask him what to do with a computer printout. He realized he was unable to name the experiment it referred to, although he knew exactly which one it was, nor could he say the words "printout," "experiment," or "data" despite the fact that he used these words quite frequently. When he turned to the computer to log-off, he was unable to remember the command "logoff." Although he was not particularly worried at his inability to locate these words, he realized something was wrong and tested his physical abilities by walking to the bathroom and back. He called home and, because he was speaking hesitantly, his wife asked if he was okay. He said, "I guess I'm confused," but was unable to explain how he could no longer remember words. After he started several sentences with non-substantive words, e.g. "well, we were," his wife insisted that he be driven to a hospital.

About 40 minutes after the beginning of the incident, just as he was about to leave his office with his assistant, he looked at the computer and now found he could log-off easily. Also, the words he had been looking for returned and he said them aloud to himself to assure himself that he could. In the hospital, it was determined that an arterio-venous malformation in the anterior left temporal lobe had diverted blood from nearby brain tissue, thus resulting in the transient anomia. In anomic aphasia, then, relatively small lesions anywhere within the language area are seen to result in difficulty finding specific substantive words. Syntax remains unimpaired, however, and comprehension is quite spared.

Other cortical syndromes

In addition to Broca's, Wernicke's, and conduction aphasia, other standard syndromes include "pure word deafness," "alexia," "transcortical motor aphasia" and "transcortical sensory aphasia. Pure word deafness is an inability to make sense of oral language in a person with normal hearing. Asked "What did you eat for breakfast?" the patient may respond "Breakfast. Breakfast? It sounds familiar but it doesn't speak to me." This syndrome results from an injury to Heschl's gyrus. Similarly, when visual linguistic stimuli are not processed due to injury to the angular gyrus, the resulting deficit is called "alexia." The pure alexic can speak and understand language well but can no longer read. (See chapter 9.)

Transcortical motor aphasia and transcortical sensory aphasia parallel Broca's and Wernicke's aphasias respectively. However, in the transcortical syndromes, repetition is entirely spared because the lesions are beyond ("trans") the language area. Patients with transcortical motor aphasia will initiate little language and what they say will be fragmentary although not agrammatic (e.g. Examiner: Can you tell me the story of what brought you to the hospital? Patient: A stroke). Their comprehension is relatively spared. Patients with transcortical sensory aphasia have poor comprehension and fluent but semantically empty speech, except when they are repeating, of course.

Subcortical aphasias

We have metaphorically "only touched the surface" in our discussion of language deficits after brain damage so far. We have presented each of the aphasias above in terms of damage to the cortex or "gray matter." However, as we saw in chapter 3, there are a number of subcortical ("white matter") areas thought to be involved in normal language. Characteristic of the subcortical aphasics is the clinicians' inability to decide if the patients are "fluent" or "non-fluent." Such patients do not produce large amounts of language uninterruptedly and with exuberance, as a Wernicke's aphasic will; their speech is sparse and slowed, although grammatically correct.

Alexander and Naeser (1988) describe a set of subcortical aphasias associated with damage to different subcortical structures. Patients with lesions in the insula/internal capsule area show a mild fluent aphasia, similar to conduction aphasia, with phonemic substitutions (e.g. *hand* pronounced as /hæld/) especially in repetition and oral reading. These authors describe symptoms similar to those of transcortical motor aphasia in patients with white matter damage farther forward in the brain. Such patients appear to have an intact grammar, but they have sparse output. They seem to have lost the "drive to speak." The authors show that auditory comprehension deficits may result from lesions in the temporal isthmus (see Figure 2.6). Finally, they point out that with enough subcortical damage a patient may even be globally aphasic. Alexander and Naeser note that many previously confusing findings with respect to symptoms and lesion site may become understandable with reference to subcortical damage. For example, a patient with agrammatic production and a lesion in Broca's area may show comprehension deficits more usually found in Wernicke's aphasia as a result of damage to the temporal isthmus, because that connects Wernicke's area to Broca's area.

Special patterns in aphasia

All of the questions of brain maturation and brain representation for language become more complex when we consider other populations. For example, speakers of a visual-gestural language must process and produce spatial information, often considered to be a right hemisphere function. Does this lead to more significant right hemisphere involvement in speech/language?

The weight of evidence in the literature would seem to support similar but not identical brain representation for signed and spoken languages. Corina et al. (1992) report on their study of a left-lesioned, native signer (WL). Although WL's post-stroke ability to pantomime and interpret *gestures* was essentially intact, he demonstrated marked aphasic symptoms in his signing. He had a Wernicke's-type aphasia with comprehension difficulties, neologisms and paraphasias parallel to those found in hearing patients.

Paul D., another aphasic signer reported on in Vaid and Corina (1989), had more Broca-like symptoms, with frequent, missing inflection. This patient also experienced intrusions by his left hand in signing, suggesting possible right-hemisphere influence.

J. Sarno et al. (1969) report the case of aphasia in a man deaf from birth who had acquired some speech through his five years of schooling in a school that promotes oral language for the deaf, as well as some American Sign Language and finger spelling. At the age of 69, he had a stroke that resulted in severe aphasia, apparently from anterior brain damage. Like a hearing individual with this sort of lesion, his comprehension in all modalities was better than his production. As a Broca's aphasic might point to his mouth in frustration that it does not say what he wants, this patient would point to his right hand. Indeed, like most bilingual aphasics (see chapter 10) his ability in his various modalities seemed to be proportionate to his abilities before the aphasia-producing stroke: he was best at signs, not so good at finger spelling, and particularly poor at lip-reading which had been his poorest modality before his stroke. As to his production of language, speaking was worst, writing and finger spelling were medial. Combining signs, finger spelling, and a bit of vocalization worked best for him.

Bilingual speakers are another population for whom the question of unusual brain organization has been raised. If a person grows up with two languages, do the two languages share "brain space"? Do the same left-hemisphere regions important for monolingual linguistic abilities support bilinguals' languages as well? Might the right hemisphere be more involved in language perception/production by bilinguals? Do people who begin learning a second language later than the first acquire similar brain representation? After brain damage do the two or more languages manifest the same sort of aphasia? We postpone a more full discussion of these issues until chapter 10.

Women aphasics constitute another "unusual" group, since so much of our knowledge about aphasia derives from war injuries and strokes, both more common in men than women. McGlone (1977) and Kimura (1983, 1993) have argued that incidence of aphasia is somewhat less in women than in men, even when the lesser incidence of stroke among women is accounted for. Kimura and Harshman (1984) have also reported that the language area in women seems to be somewhat anterior to that of men. However, many studies find no differences between aphasia type or lesion size between the two genders (e.g. M. T. Sarno et al., 1985, Kertesz and Benke, 1989).

Hier et al. (1994) found small gender differences in aphasia following stroke, consistent with Kimura's notion. Also, Broca's aphasia was more frequent in men while the fluent aphasias (Wernicke's aphasia and anomic aphasia) *and* global aphasia were more frequent in women. Moreover the size of the brain damage required to result in aphasia was greater for men than for women, suggesting somewhat more diffuse organization of language in them (although this could relate to larger overall brain size – due to larger overall body size – for men as well); the authors note that the size of stroke damage on average was the same in men and women. In sum, the results are not in on subtle differences that may obtain in aphasia type and location between the genders.

Conclusion

The different aphasia syndromes are linked to damage in different areas of the central left hemisphere. Problems in coming up with specific lexical items arise with mild damage anywhere within the "language area" around the Sylvian fissure. Problems with producing the sounds of language correctly and in generating syntactic strings of words are associated with predominantly anterior lesions including Broca's area. Problems with comprehension and "empty" speech are associated with damage to posterior regions around Wernicke's area. Problems with repetition can arise with damage to either of these areas, but problems exclusively or predominantly with repetition arise when the pathways between the two areas are damaged. Damage to subcortical structures that underlie the language areas can also result in aphasia by cutting links crucial for producing language.

5 Aphasia: what underlies the syndromes

The previous chapter gave a general overview of the types of symptoms seen in aphasia. We discussed some early ideas about what these symptoms meant for theories of brain representation for language. More modern research has allowed us a closer look at injured brains in live patients and a more developed, theoretical basis for creating language tests for aphasic patients. In this chapter we consider the explanations that have been suggested for agrammatism, Wernicke's aphasia, the diagnostic dichotomy *fluent*: *non-fluent*, and conduction aphasia.

Agrammatism

A subset of patients with Broca's aphasia fit the criteria for agrammatism that is, speech which is essentially devoid of appropriately used closed class or function words. The speech of these patients is generally slow and effortful. Some may also have phonetic difficulties. Early research on the nature of the deficit in agrammatism referred only to these production problems. More recent studies have turned up subtle comprehension deficits as well. Not all patients experience the same problems to the same extent. For this reason, there is some disagreement about the status of agrammatism. Some researchers say it is a collection of unrelated symptoms each of which might be more profitably studied separately. Others consider the production deficits definitional and are unconcerned with the other aspects of agrammatics' linguistic abilities. Still others attempt explanations which would account for all of the observed symptoms.

Consider the questions that arise from speech samples such as that in chapter 4 from L.M., the patient with Broca's aphasia. Recall that he makes frequent pauses and shows some transient difficulty with articulation ("can ... candy"). Might all of his difficulties be attributed to an inability to reliably activate the neurons needed to move the speech muscles? He also shows some lexical disturbances, however. In fact he says the word "candy" when he wants to say "cookie." When the examiner asks him about what the woman was doing with the dishes, and the answer is "washing them" he says "discharge my .. I forgot .. dirtying clothes." It is possible that he is simply having trouble remembering the words he wants. Alternatively, perhaps the representations for many words in his lexicon are now incomplete. In that case, a lack of subcategorization frames – information about what sorts of nouns verbs must take – might account for L.M.'s inability to produce well-formed sentences.

Different parts of speech seem differentially affected. While he has some whole phrases, they are formulae, e.g. "well, I don't know." When he is actually trying to describe the picture, he is much more likely to use verbs and nouns, rather than modifiers or functor words. Does this mean that these word categories were formerly stored in different brain areas? Or does their different rate of occurrence in L.M.'s speech result from a difference in the roles of, say, nouns and adjectives or prepositions and nouns in some post-lexical stage of speech production?

Finally, we noted that L.M. did not experience difficulty in comprehending everyday conversations but performed poorly on tests of understanding complex syntax. For example, if he were asked "The lion was killed by the tiger; who died?" he is more likely to pick the tiger than the lion. To what extent do his comprehension difficulties parallel his production problems? Do phonological features of words play a role in his comprehension problems? Can he understand words he is unable to produce in confrontation naming tasks? Are there syntactic constructions not found in his free speech yet comprehensible to him? A brief discussion of some specific approaches to agrammatism should illustrate the progress made in understanding the effects of lesions resulting in Broca's aphasia, as well as the extent of disagreement as to the proper interpretation of the linguistic disturbances in non-fluent aphasia.

Analysis of the sound patterns in the speech of Broca's aphasics is perhaps the simplest place to begin. It is generally agreed that most of the sound errors in Broca's aphasia result from difficulties in the end stage(s) of speech production. There may be some distortion in the quality of speech sounds. This is referred to as "dysarthria." There may also be some blurring of important distinctions in the patient's language. For example, Blumstein et al. (1977) investigated the voice onset time (VOT, the time when the vocal cords start vibrating relative to the release of the stop) for voiced (e.g. [b]) and voiceless (e.g. [p]) stop sounds in patients classified as Broca's or Wernicke's aphasics. They found that whereas normal speakers and Wernicke's aphasics showed no overlap of onset times across series of voiced and voiceless stops, Broca's aphasics did not have this "buffer zone." Broca's aphasics were inconsistent; for some of their voiceless targets, they actually started their vocal cords vibrating earlier than for some of their voiced sounds.

One interesting attempt at locating all of the symptoms of Broca's aphasia in a single linguistic component was Kean's 1977 theory that agrammatism resulted from a phonological deficit. Kean analyzed the language produced by Broca's aphasics and their comprehension difficulties. She found that the words that created the most difficulties for these patients were those which the phonological component of the grammar did not treat as full-fledged words. Although prepositions, articles and other so-called "function words" do not form a coherent morphological or syntactic class, they are demonstrably different from "content words" phonologically. They generally do not attract stress in a sentence and they undergo some of the same low-level phonetic processes (e.g. vowel reduction) in English. If a Broca's aphasic's linguistic system were only able to deal with full-fledged phonological words, then the patient would omit grammatical markers (whether bound or free morphologically) in production and ignore them in processing. Although this theory was an important contribution, it was abandoned as evidence accumulated that few languages (English and the other languages considered by Kean in her analysis) had this parallel dichotomy of phonological words/non-words and function/content words.

One of the directions taken by researchers in morphological and/or syntactic aspects of agrammatism is to look for dissociations of the various symptoms of the syndrome. Linebarger, Schwartz, and Saffran (1983) studied the ability of agrammatic patients with deficits in comprehension and production and found them surprisingly unimpaired on a grammaticality judgment task. The authors interpreted these results as evidence for agrammatics' preserved syntactic competence; instead, they suggested, agrammatics have a disruption in the assignment of thematic roles to sentence constituents.

Grammaticality judgment tasks generally involve decisions as to the well-formedness of a string after the subject has read or listened to the string. This is different from the usual process of sentence comprehension which must happen as the sentence is being produced. A number of researchers have designed tasks which evaluate the morphological and syntactic "on-line" processing of sentences by aphasic patients.

A 1987 paper by Tyler and Cobb presents the results of a linguistic experiment conducted with their agrammatic patient DE. In this experiment they asked DE to listen for words in sentences and timed how long it took him to respond. Immediately before the word DE was to listen for, there occurred one of three wordtypes: a complex word consisting of a root plus contextually appropriate suffix (e.g. "waste*ful*" cook), a complex word consisting of a root plus contextually inappropriate suffix (e.g. "wast*age*" cook) or a root-suffix combination which resulted in a non-word (e.g. "wastely"). The suffixes were of two types: derivational – changing the part of speech, e.g. writ*er*, and inflectional – contributing syntactic information, e.g. write*s*.

When unimpaired subjects did this task, they were slower to find the words when they came after inappropriate suffixes, presumably because they spent some time trying to integrate the peculiar suffix into the sentence context. Since unimpaired subjects have access to both the syntactic information which determines the presence of inflectional endings and morphological information which determines the presence of derivational endings, it is not surprising that this difference was apparent for both derivational and inflectional suffixes.

When DE attempted these word-finding tasks, his responses were fast and accurate, well within normal limits. But his pattern of delays was unlike that of the normal subjects. For derivational suffixes, DE took significantly more time to report having found the target word when it came after inappropriately suffixed words than after appropriately suffixed words. However, after inflectional suffixes, DE showed no difference between appropriate and inappropriate suffixes. If it is true that words with derivational suffixes are listed separately in the mental dictionary whereas inflectional suffixes are listed apart from any roots they might attach to and are simply added on to roots because of the syntactic context in which the root appears, then it would seem that the damage caused by DE's accident has selectively disturbed the lexical representation for inflectional suffixes.[2]

In much the same way that Tyler used an on-line task to test DE's sensitivity to morphological facts about English, Baum (1989) tested the sensitivity of a group of Broca's aphasics to syntactic properties of English. Baum compared the ability of normals and aphasics to listen for target words in long and short sentences. Some of the long sentences and some of the short sentences involved local dependencies (i.e. relationships between constituents in the same clause). The rest of the long and short sentences contained long-distance (across clause boundary) dependencies. Normals showed grammaticality effects in both local and long-distance types. That is, they took longer to respond to words that occurred in ungrammatical contexts than they did to respond to words that occurred in grammatical contexts. The syntactic structure they were building facilitated their word-monitoring. The seven Broca's aphasics in this experiment showed grammaticality effects only in sentences where the crucial context was a local dependency. This could be due to the fact that local violations were not exclusively syntactic; they were also morphological or lexical. It could be because the long-distance dependencies always involved syntactic gaps. Grodzinsky (1984) had posited that, for agrammatics who had syntactic problems with comprehension, these arose from the inability to process syntactic traces of items that have been referred to earlier in a sentence. Either way, the fact that these aphasics show on-line sensitivity to material which is problematic in their production and/or comprehension is indicative of a processing deficit rather than a structural deficit.

Agrammatics have also been shown to be sensitive to certain syntactic properties of the very "closed-class" elements which are so often missing or misused in their production. Shankweiler et al. (1989) provided evidence of such sensitivity in an on-line task. They asked aphasics and normal controls to judge the grammaticality of sentences and determine the location of any ungrammaticality. The violations were of two types. One involved the substitution of an inappropriate, closed-class word of the same syntactic category (e.g. The good-natured baker put *at* a white hat). In the other type an inappropriate closed-class word of a different syntactic category was substituted (The good-natured baker put *is* a silk scarf). Overall, the aphasics had lower accuracy and longer response times than the controls. This could reflect either a loss of the relevant structures or a deficit in linguistic processing. However, the aphasic and control groups showed similar patterns of response times and accuracy to the two violation types. Both groups were sensitive to this difference. Again, this argues for preserved syntactic knowledge in the agrammatic patients.

Similarly, Blumstein et al. (1991) show that the Broca's aphasics in their experiment were building syntactic structure as they attempted to process sentences in a lexical decision task. The patients' decisions about whether a particular set of letters constituted an English word were significantly slower when the target was found in an ungrammatical setting.

If agrammatic aphasics are attempting to build syntactic structure in processing sentences, what explanations might there be for the impoverished structure of their speech? Zingeser and Berndt (1990) – see also Berndt et al., 1997a and 1997b – suggest that agrammatics may have particular difficulty with verb retrieval in production and thus more trouble with sentence structure since they are not getting subcategorization information. They compare agrammatics to anomics who have a specific difficulty in retrieving nouns. Since nouns do not carry information about particular complements necessary for creating grammatical sentences, the production of patients with anomia remains fairly fluent.

Nouns and verbs do, however, differ in other ways as well. Joanette and Goulet (1991) suggested that the difficulty experienced by agrammatic aphasics in producing verbs may be more appropriately considered a text-level difficulty at the point where sentences are constructed about things (noun phrases: NPs) and what they do (verb phrases: VPs). Verbs carry a greater part of the information in a sentence. They determine which NPs may serve as their subjects (selection restrictions) and which complements are required (subcategorization). Agrammatics may find the more propositional verbs more difficult than the relatively non-propositional nouns.

Berndt and Zingeser (1991) reply that the text-level model that Joanette and Goulet proposed is a discourse-processing model, not a model of sentence production. Since any non-noun might have a propositional function in some discourse unit, it is difficult to see how such a text-level analysis might explain word-class differences in retrieval. The conflicting frameworks within which the two sets of authors work do not allow for a direct comparison, but it is certainly conceivable that both syntactic category and discourse function play significant roles in agrammatic production.

Each of the papers discussed in this section presents a particular dissociation of abilities in agrammatic patients. Specifically, dissociations have been found between comprehension and production difficulties, between a combined comprehension/production difficulty and preserved knowledge of grammaticality, and between various aspects of on-line processing. Taken together, this body of work (along with many other studies not discussed here) points toward a preserved syntactic competence in agrammatism with difficulties arising from damage to only some aspects of processing or production mechanisms.

Not all researchers would agree with this conclusion. Some believe that the evidence suggests that "agrammatism" should not be considered a syndrome. Instead, each of the symptoms, since they are dissociable, should be considered separately.

A particularly interesting set of dissociations is reported by

Caramazza and Miceli (1991) in the comprehension and production of a *fluent* aphasic whose initials are E.B. When asked to point to which of two pictures represents a spoken or written sentence, E.B. had severely impaired ability to assign thematic role – to decide which noun in a sentence is the doer, and which the done-to – in active and, especially, passive sentences. This is similar to the analysis offered for the non-fluent patients in Linebarger et al. (1985). However, phonologically and morphologically, E.B.'s production is essentially normal. The patient's performance on a well-formedness judgment task is also normal. Hence there is a double dissociation of asyntactic comprehension and difficulty in processing closed-class elements. The authors reject the explanation of a simple role-assigning heuristic (e.g. "Make the first noun the agent"). They point out that this would lead to incorrect assignments in what are called non-reversible passives, that is, sentences like "The ice-cream was eaten by the boy," where it is not possible that the boy was eaten by the ice-cream, as well as in the reversible passives (e.g. "The man was pushed by the woman") where errors are actually found. The authors suggest that the actual *representation* of (some) verbs is disturbed in this patient and presumably in other patients with these types of comprehension problems, even though they have frontal lesions and the non-fluent production and relatively spared comprehension usually associated with Broca's aphasia.

Arguments against agrammatism as an aphasia syndrome are also made without appeal to fluent aphasics. Some researchers who have looked at differences in the production and comprehension of non-fluent patients who are speakers of languages other than English have concluded that the differences from language to language are greater than the differences among aphasia types within a single language. For example, in languages where inflectional endings carry more semantic weight than they do in English, non-fluent aphasics omit them less often. (Miceli et al. 1989, Bates et al. 1987, Bates, Wulfeck and MacWhinney 1991.)

One strong proponent of agrammatism as a theoretically coherent category has been David Caplan (1991). He does not deny the variability in the difficulties experienced by agrammatic patients (c.f. Miceli et al. 1989) but rather he claims that this variability is a result of the broadness of the category "agrammatism." His claim is that there is evidence to suggest that although function words and inflectional morphemes, which are both frequently omitted in the speech of non-fluent aphasics, do not form a syntactic class, there are production mechanisms – yet to be fully described – that treat them similarly.

Grodzinsky (1991) also defends researchers' attempts to make generalizations about agrammatic patients' data. He points out that both clinical and theoretical definitions of agrammatism refer to types of omissions and substitutions, NOT to quantities of omissions and substitutions. As to the suggestion that the relationship between comprehension and production deficits in agrammatism is unpredictable enough to weaken the hypothesis of a single, underlying deficit, Grodzinsky replies that when only those patients who have both non-fluent speech and a paucity of morphosyntactic markers in their speech are considered, the relationship becomes more predictable.

Although Grodzinsky argues for the coherence of agrammatism as a syndrome, he does not agree that syntactic competence is spared with impaired production mechanisms causing the typical difficulties. He asserts that the central deficit in agrammatism is what is called the deletion of traces. Consider the sentence "The girl was pushed by the boy." It can be diagrammed thus if we assume **t** stands for the trace left behind when a word has been moved from its position in an underlying sentence:

[The girl]$_i$ was pushed $\mathbf{t}_i$ by [the boy].

The sentence derives from "The boy pushed the girl." We understand that the NP "the girl" is the object of the verb "push," in this theory, because it left behind a trace, here labelled "**t**" when it moved from object position. If that trace were deleted in agrammatism, the noun phrase "the girl" would be considered the "doer" rather than "done to" as the first noun in a sentence usually is the "agent."

Clearly the phenomenon of agrammatism forms the crux of several important arguments in neurolinguistics today: (1) whether it even exists as a unified phenomenon, (2) if it does, whether it reflects actual grammatical breakdown, (3) if so, what grammatical principles and/or structures are affected. Because the field has many researchers debating these questions currently, it is hard to tell when or how these questions will be resolved.

Wernicke's aphasia

In reviewing some of the approaches to the analysis of agrammatic production and comprehension, we see that no one theory is perfectly able to account for all of the data presented. Descriptively, however, it remains clear that there are some robust differences between the speech of Broca's aphasics with more anterior lesions and that of the Wernicke's aphasics with more posterior lesions. Even in cross-language studies aimed at finding similarities between anterior and posterior aphasics, such as Bates, Wulfeck and MacWhinney (1991), "subtle processing differences" between Broca's and Wernicke's aphasics are found.

The linguistic deficits in Wernicke's aphasia tend to be more lexical-semantic. In a study of the sorts of substitution errors made by aphasic patients, Ardila and Rosselli (1993) find that substitutions of an individual phoneme within a word occur only in patients with lesions close to the Sylvian fissure, that is Broca's aphasics (who make a lot of them), conduction aphasics, and Wernicke's aphasics. (These aphasics, as it happens, were speakers of Spanish, although there is no reason to believe that this finding would not hold equally for speakers of other languages.) Patients with anomic aphasias tended to have smaller posterior lesions than Wernicke's aphasics. They made virtually no phonemic paraphasias (substitutions of individual phonemes) and primarily semantic, verbal paraphasias. The Wernicke's aphasics, by contrast, with sizable posterior lesions, made both phonemic paraphasias and neologisms, that is non-words where the target word is unrecognizable. The lesions of the Wernicke's patients also extended higher than those of the anomics, on average. Patients with lesions outside what is traditionally considered the "language area," that is transcortical motor aphasics with lesions in the frontal lobe, made extremely few substitutions. Such an analysis confirms our notion that the language area around the Sylvian fissure is crucial for production of lexical items. Posterior regions within this area are required for generating target words themselves; the entire path must be available for speaking the entire string of phonemes in the appropriate order.

Recall the sample of speech from A.M. in the previous chapter. His discourse is called "empty," in part, because it is repetitious, but also, more importantly, because it contains "words" – really phoneme strings – that are not words in English, like *taenz*. This phenomenon, associated with posterior aphasics, is called *neologistic jargon*. In their book on the topic, Buckingham and Kertesz cite a severely impaired patient, B.F., who answered the examiner's question "Who is running the store now?" with the following:

> "I don't know. Yes, the bick, uh, yes I would say that the mick daysis nosis or chpickters. Course, I have also missed on the carfter teck. Do you know what that is? I've, uh, token to ingish. They have been toast sosilly. They'd have been put to myafa and made palis and, uh, myadakal senda you. That is me alordisdus. That makes anacronous senda." (Buckingham and Kertesz, 1976: 21.)

At a few points in such a paragraph we think we know what the target is (e.g. when the patient says *ingish* we suspect he may be commenting on his problems with English). At other points, it is unclear whether he is even responding to the question that was asked. Some aphasiologists believe that patients indeed have targets in mind, but are entirely unable to reach them in production, and due to the severe comprehension deficits are unable to monitor their own output, that is, to realize it does not make sense and needs to be corrected. Butterworth (1979), by contrast, suggests that there is a "random phoneme generator" operating that kicks in when target words cannot be found, yet the speaker feels the need to speak.

Note that functor words and inflectional affixes are produced in abundance in Wernicke's aphasia. However, the two instances of "paragrammatism" that can be seen in the passage in the previous chapter ("work of nothing else" and "the doctor find me") do indicate that A.M.'s syntax is at least "slightly off."

Wernicke's aphasics' comprehension is more impaired than their production. They would have trouble, for example, answering a simple question from The Boston Diagnostic Aphasia Exam such as "Does a good pair of rubber boots keep water out?" Of course, to say that a patient's comprehension is relatively more impaired than that same patient's production is not to say anything at all about the severity of the comprehension deficit. Comprehension can be measured in a number of semantic tasks. Naming of pictures of objects and/or actions may be impaired. Patients may be unable to point to a written representation of orally presented words.

Zurif and Caramazza (1976) established that their Wernicke's patients' ability to make judgments about the relatedness of words was severely impaired. Their task consisted of groups of three words, only two of which would normally be considered semantically related (e.g. husband-turtle-wife). Their patients' choices about which two of the three words went best together was essentially random. However, just as was the case with Broca's aphasics, tasks that involve on-line access of semantic information demonstrate that, although perhaps not available for conscious reflection, patients do retain much knowledge of semantic category.

Tyler (1988) reports that fluent aphasics with impaired comprehension show evidence of the ability to build syntactic structure in on-line tasks. She created a task in which subjects listened for target words in three different types of "sentences." Some were normal sentences. Others were semantically anomalous but syntactically well formed, like Chomsky's famous example "Colorless green ideas sleep furiously." The third type was a scrambled string with no semantic or syntactic structure. We know that normals find words in such a task faster when the words come later in a sentence; the syntactic structure they are building makes the task easier. This is called the "word-position effect." Tyler's fluent aphasic subjects showed word-position effects for the normal sentences and the anomalous ones but not for the scrambled ones. This suggests that they, like the normals, were aided in the word-finding task by the syntactic structure they were building. The only sentences for which they did not show a word-position effect were precisely those which had no syntactic structure (i.e. the scrambled sentences).

If there is spared ability in Wernicke's aphasics to construct syntactic structures, why then do we see the strange structures of paragrammatism? Deeper aspects of structure may be spared while surface aspects may be impaired. The severe difficulty Wernicke's aphasics have in choosing meaningful, lexical items in their speech renders it hard for us to be sure they intend to produce interpretable propositions, however.

An alternative distinction between non-fluent and fluent aphasics

Jakobson (1941 and 1968) pointed out an alternate way to contrast non-fluent Broca's aphasics with Wernicke's fluent aphasics. His idea derives from the notions that de Saussure developed, distinguishing paradigmatic from syntagmatic aspects of language. Recall that words that are syntagmatically related can occur right next to each other, as in "President Clinton" or "Queen Elizabeth" or "John walked." Words that are paradigmatically related to each other can substitute for each other; words like "president" and "queen" and "officer" are all paradigmatically related; as are words like "he," "it," and "they." As Luria described the problem in 1973, appropriate choice of phonemes and words is a paradigmatic activity because one can select any of a number of possible candidates, while the constructing of these words into sentences is a syntagmatic activity. Thus patients who make literal paraphasias, substituting one or two phonemes into a word, or patients who misselect words, tend to be the patients with posterior brain damage, while patients with problems constructing sentences will be patients with anterior brain damage and non-fluent aphasia.

Luria is quite explicit in linking these "Two Basic Kinds of Aphasic Disorders" (the article's title) to lesion localization; disorders of paradigmatic systems are associated with posterior regions in the language area. Disturbances in the left temporal lobe cortex bring about breakdown in what he calls the *phonematic code*; disturbance in the parietal lobe results in problems with organization of articulatory processes. Disturbance at the temporo-parieto-occipital junction in the left hemisphere results in sparing of the paradigmatic systems for phonemes and articulation, but problems in what Luria terms the semantic system, that is the system responsible for lexical selection. As a consequence, the patient substitutes incorrect words for the target words. All these types of lesions do not result in any problems in the syntagmatic system; those problems are the result of more anterior lesions. With brain damage in anterior speech areas, by contrast, paradigmatic abilities such as phoneme selection and lexical selection are relatively spared, while the ability to construct words into sentences is impaired.

Conduction aphasia

In the previous chapter, we discussed a particular kind of aphasic syndrome in which the principal difficulty is neither production nor comprehension but rather repetition. This syndrome, conduction aphasia, was, we mentioned, previously attributed to a damaged arcuate fasciculus, the structure thought to be responsible for "conducting" information from the comprehension area (i.e. Wernicke's area) to the production area (i.e. Broca's area). Our modern imaging techniques have shown us that not all patients who have a particular difficulty with repetition have damage to the arcuate fasciculus.

Most striking, in addition to the inability to repeat, is conduction aphasics' phonemic paraphasias, that is, their substitution of phonemes within their target word. Characteristically, the conduction aphasic will approach the target word in successive attempts: e.g., Goodglass gives the following example of a patient trying to name a whistle "tris . . . chi . . . twissle" (Goodglass, 1993, page 142). It would appear that the patient has information about the target lexicon in mind, but is unable to assemble it in production. Indeed, Kohn (1984 and 1992) has suggested that the problem lies in the stage of "programming" the motor articulation of the planned word. Conduction aphasics, unlike Wernicke's aphasics, are distressed in their awareness that they have not succeeded in producing the correct word.

Pate, Saffran, and Morton (1987) examined the errors made by one conduction aphasic, NU, in great detail. In tasks like oral reading, NU produced many phonemic paraphasias (e.g.

[tɛvəlɪʃə] for television). In addition, he often left out unstressed syllables in longer words. However, in metalinguistic tasks, NU was able to tell words from non-words even when the non-words were created in ways that mimicked his errors in repetition. He was within normal, adult range on a syllable-counting test. Also, NU often correctly pronounced his target word after several attempts. These facts indicate that the phonological representations of words in NU's lexicon were probably intact. Interestingly, the great majority of NU's errors occurred inside words. In fact, he was more likely to make errors on a single four-syllable word than on a multi-word unit of eight or more syllables! Clearly the word is an important unit in NU's phonological planning with errors occurring as he attempts to put phonemes into the appropriate positions.

The current perspective on comprehension and production as complex phenomena has encouraged researchers to consider the errors made by conduction aphasics as evidence for a disruption at a specific level of language production. The most frequent level suggested is probably the "positional level" of a production model such as that described in Garrett (1980), that is, the level at which phonemes are placed into position in a word. In his model of sentence structure, much referred to in neurolinguistic work, this level follows the functional level at which basic substantives necessary to express a sentence's meaning have been selected. At the positional level, a sentence frame, including functors, is generated and the substantives are actually composed.

Conclusion

The phenomena dealt with in this chapter – agrammatism associated with Broca's aphasia, lexical substitutions associated with Wernicke's aphasia, and phonemic substitutions associated with conduction aphasia – can each be linked to a particular brain area that, when damaged, results in the deficit. These areas are, of course, respectively, the areas in and around Broca's area, Wernicke's area, and the arcuate fasciculus. By a standard neuropsychological line of reasoning, we assume that if a specific language behavior stands out as particularly impaired when others are spared, this dissociation means the area in question is crucial for performance of that language behavior in normals. Thus neurolinguists conclude that Broca's area is crucial for production of syntactically fleshed-out sentences, Wernicke's area is crucial for producing meaningful speech (as well as for comprehension), and the arcuate fasciculus (or, in Luria's theory, the parietal lobe) is necessary for stringing phonemes into the words they compose.

6 Childhood aphasia and other language disorders

Many linguists believe that the ability to acquire language is innate. These linguists point out that there are universal principles of how human language is structured (e.g., all languages will have adjectives as well as nouns) and, in addition, there are language-specific factors or parameters (such as the fact that adjectives precede the nouns they modify in English but follow them in Spanish). Infants' brains are, presumably, structured so that they will easily learn exactly how the universal elements are expressed in the language(s) they are exposed to, and pick up the language-specific features as well.

But how is the brain involved? By the time these infants become adults their left hemisphere will be primarily responsible for language organization and processing. A number of electrophysiological techniques have been used to demonstrate that the left hemisphere is dominant for language in early infancy before language is learned (e.g. Mills, Coffey-Corina, and Neville, 1993). We might then ask ourselves whether the left hemisphere controls language even in the very young. The data from childhood aphasia provide a partial answer to this question. First we must distinguish two sorts of language disturbance in childhood, language disturbance that results from sudden brain damage, as in the case of a car accident, and developmental dysphasia, that is, the inability to acquire language or aspects of language due to some brain damage before or around birth.

Aphasia in childhood

In some ways the aphasias of childhood are similar to those of adulthood. One sees an immediate interruption in the language abilities of whatever stage of language development the child has achieved at the time of the accident. In the child, however, unlike the adult, substantial recovery takes place following brain injury. Interestingly, the patterns of aphasia seen in childhood are not exactly like those of adulthood. Most strikingly, there are virtually no reports of the "fluent" aphasias in children. Rather, even when the damage is to an area that in an adult would be associated with a Wernicke's aphasia, that is, a posterior lesion, the child will produce slow effortful speech with reduced syntactic complexity if not outright agrammatism.

Lenneberg (1967) studied children with unilateral brain injury to analyze its effects on language, language development, and lateralization. His results are summarized in Table 6.1. Since infants were able to sustain significant brain damage and still acquire language normally, Lenneberg concluded that the two hemispheres are initially equally able to control language. This is known as the "equipotentiality" hypothesis. He also noted that the age at which persistent aphasic symptoms resulted from left-hemisphere injury was approximately the same age, around puberty, at which "foreign accents" became likely in second language acquisition. He proposed that the brain had a certain interval when its plasticity allowed for the flawless acquisition of language. During this time, new brain areas could assume the functions of injured areas. This is known as the "critical period hypothesis." Since Lenneberg proposed this hypothesis in 1967, numerous researchers have tested it to find out when the critical period ends. A particularly convincing study is that by Johnson and Newport (1989) that tested grammaticality judgment in a large group of subjects who had immigrated to the United States at different ages. When tested around a decade after their arrival, a clear decline in abilities was seen starting in people who arrived as early as age five, for certain syntactic phenomena.

Moreover more recent studies suggest that the right hemisphere is not entirely able to take over language functions, even in childhood. There is neuroanatomical evidence to explain why this is. Maureen Dennis and her colleagues, for example, studied the language of people aged eight to twenty-eight who had had their right or left hemisphere removed six or more years previously. On the surface, the language of children who had had left-brain damage in early childhood looked normal as they participated in daily conversation or school. However grammatical tests such as choosing the correct picture out of two for reversible passives revealed below-normal performance (Dennis and Kohn, 1975).

They may, for example, avoid the passive construction in production. On tests of comprehension of complex constructions, they may tend to interpret the first noun phrase in a sentence as the agent or doer of the action, even in passives and other constructions where this is not the correct interpretation. These children are able to correctly interpret sentences with unusual word order when the roles of the sentential subject and object are pragmatically clear, such as in:

> *John* ate the sandwich.   *John* correctly given *agent* role.
> *The sandwich* was eaten by John.   *John* still the agent.

However, in so-called reversible passives, where the only cue about roles comes from the grammatical markers, problems of interpretation occur:

> Dana kissed Val. vs. Dana was kissed by Val.
> *Dana* was assigned the agent role in both cases.

As to the critical age hypothesis, based on a carefully selected series of brain-damaged children, speech-language pathologist Dorothy Aram (1988) challenges earlier work that showed differences between brain injury in the time around birth as compared to later in early childhood. She asserts that when proper patient selection criteria are used, the only important differences in language outcome years after the injury stem from the particular hemisphere injured and perhaps from the particular lesion site within the hemisphere. She analyzed the spontaneous speech of left- and right-hemisphere-damaged children and that of normal controls matched for such factors as age, sex, and socio-economic status as well as certain non-neurological health factors. She

Table 6.1. *Summary of linguistic and neurolinguistic development (adapted with permission from Eric H. Lenneberg's* Biological Foundations of Language)

Age	Usual language development	Effect on language of left lateral lesions	Other remarks
0–3 months	– Emergence of cooing	– No effect in 50% of cases; 50% with delayed onset (but normal development)	– No lateralization of function
4–20 months	– from babbling to words		
21–36 months	– Acquisition of language structure	– All language accomplishments disappear; language is reacquired with repetition of all stages	– Hand preference emerges – Left hemisphere begins to assume sole responsibility for language – Language appears to involve whole brain
3–10 years	– Grammatical refinement and expansion of vocabulary	– Aphasic symptoms; tendency for full recovery (except in reading and/or writing)	– Evidence for both hemispheres still active in language; right/left lateral-lesion disrupts language – Possible to re-establish language in right hemisphere if left is damaged

11–14 years	– Foreign accents in 2nd language learning	– Some aphasic symptoms are not reversible, particularly in traumatic lesions	– Lateralization is formally established – usually irreversibly – Language-free parts of brain cannot take over except where lateralization is incomplete (due to childhood pathology)
Mid-teens-senium	– Acquisition of 2nd language is increasingly difficult	– Aphasic symptoms may persist; symptoms present for more than 3–5 months are irreversible	– Language definitely lateralized in left hemisphere for 97% of population

found the speech of right-hemisphere-damaged children to be very similar to that of the non-brain-damaged controls. Left-hemisphere-damaged children had more difficulty with simple and complex sentences than did the normal controls. Both left- and right-hemisphere-damaged children showed some persistent difficulty in naming objects. Children with left-sided injury answered questions more slowly but more accurately than children with right-sided injury. Aram found no effect of age at the time of brain injury in any of her analyses. These data clearly argue against the idea of an initial state of hemispheric equipotentiality.

Anatomical studies (e.g. Galaburda and Kemper, 1979) have documented differences in the actual cell-level structure of the left and right hemispheres. The two hemispheres are not *identical* even pre-natally. Most interestingly, the left hemisphere in most people has a larger planum temporale, that is, more development on the left side of the brain in that core area of what will become the "language center." However, these structural differences do not necessarily preclude the possibility of equal potential for each hemisphere to assume language function.

On the basis of a review of the literature, Satz, Strauss, and Whitaker (1990) agree that current knowledge of neuroanatomy speaks against a complete interchangeability of the two hemispheres at birth. They suggest that Lenneberg was, however, partially correct. Their improved version of the equipotentiality hypothesis refers to the potential of left-hemisphere regions around the classical language area and right-hemisphere regions analogous to the left-hemisphere language areas to assume language functions in the event of damage to the normal left-hemisphere language areas.

Post-pubertal language acquisition

Further evidence on the critical period hypothesis comes from the studies of children acquiring language after puberty. Recall that Lenneberg predicted that it was hard to learn a second language after puberty due to crucial brain maturation being complete. By implication, individuals who were forced to acquire a first language after puberty should be equally unable to. One opportunity to study such a child was afforded scientists by the case of Genie, a child whose abusive father had Genie isolated and physically restrained day and night in a small bedroom with little light and virtually no stimulation from the age of twenty months. This abusive father so threatened Genie's mother, who was herself becoming blind, that the mother did not report the father's neglect and abuse of Genie until Genie was thirteen and a half. After this, Genie was hospitalized and treated for malnutrition, and her opportunities to socialize and learn language began.

Genie had been beaten for making any noise in the period of her tragic isolation, so she was virtually unable to vocalize when she was found. Over the next four years a linguist, Susan Curtiss (1977), was able to observe the development of her language and test how it related to her brain activity. In many ways, Genie's language development was different from that of normal children, although she certainly acquired a substantial number of linguistic rules. The phonological sounds in her early words were more varied than those of normal children and her early two syllable words were not "reduplicated," that is, consisting of a single syllable spoken twice, as are those of normal children. Also, unlike normal children, she had no early intonation patterns. While normal children learn primarily nouns at first, Genie learned verbs and adjectives as well as nouns, but delayed combining them into two-word phrases much longer than normal children. Question production remained particularly difficult for Genie over the four years Curtiss studied her, as did appropriate use of pronouns. Her acquisition of negative sentences did not follow the standard pattern; for three years she used only one structure, e.g. "no more take wax" (p. 190). In her production of language, Genie followed a fixed word-order pattern, and in her comprehension she was not able to appreciate the word-order differences that distinguish active from passive sentences. Finally, while it may be said that Genie follows rules, she treats them as much more optional than normal children do. For example, while normal children go through a period of including only full forms, and only later learn ellipsis, from the start Genie would delete subjects, verbs, or objects from sentences, whether or not the listener could appropriately infer what they were supposed to mean, e.g. "Elevator hurt silly goose."

Several different tests suggested that Genie was using primarily her right hemisphere to learn language. Dichotic tests of language showed markedly greater left-ear performance than right-ear performance. A tachistoscopic test where Genie heard rhymes and had to point to pictures she saw of a word that rhymed with the word she heard tended to show a left visual field effect as well. Also, a pilot study using evoked potentials indicated right-hemisphere differences for processing nouns and verbs.

Not only language was being processed by the right hemisphere; most of these tests suggested that non-language abilities, such as processing environmental sounds, were also being handled by Genie's right hemisphere. Curtiss points out that many aspects of language that we will see (Chapter 7) have been associated with the right hemisphere, such as formulaic speech, are not among the aspects that Genie is particularly good at. She attributes this to Genie's extreme inability to socialize, and the fact that many aspects of right-hemisphere language are pragmatic. However, Curtiss attributes Genie's difficulties with acquiring appropriate syntactic and morphosyntactic rules and her problems using them when necessary to a general right-hemisphere "holistic" thinking style that Genie evidences. She compares this to a "sequential, analytic thinking" style that we associate with normal, left-hemisphere abilities.

Of course, Genie's case is not an ideal one for testing what happens with late language acquisition because there is some question as to whether she was mentally retarded from birth and thus her father was responding so cruelly to her abnormal development. The extreme deprivation that she suffered also may have had biological influences on her brain, so it is unlikely that we see in her simply an example of "normal" delayed language acquisition. Nevertheless the case has been a valuable one for provoking us to think about the issues of how language would develop after the critical period.

Developmental dysphasia

Difficulties with language in children that are not related to one-time brain accidents are of great import for the field of speech language pathology. Among children with learning disorders, there are children with what is called specific language impairment (SLI). In these children other cognitive areas are normal or even better than normal, but language in particular is delayed abnormally. In such children no actual brain damage can be seen via any of the brain-imaging techniques, but unusual clusterings of cells have been found in some language areas of children who have died of unrelated causes.

There has been much debate in the field of childhood language disorders concerning whether there are specific subsyndromes of SLI that are primarily in production of speech or primarily in comprehension of speech. It seems that currently terms like "specific language impairment" apply to children with predominantly production problems, while children whose primary difficulties lie in making sense of language are said to have central auditory processing difficulties. A recent study employing evoked potential techniques confirms that the underlying behavioral causes for SLI differ among children. Some have difficulty with simple auditory processing while others have difficulty with simple visual processing (Neville et al., 1993).

Some children with SLI have primarily phonological problems. Their speech remains unintelligible much longer than that of normally developing children. Such children invariably make systematic errors, for example, "deleting" (i.e. of not producing) final consonants, or producing velar consonants (e.g. /k/) at a more forward point in the mouth (e.g. as /t/). Different children will consistently evidence different systematic deviations from the norm, although there are some processes that are frequent among children with phonological disorders (e.g. consonant cluster reduction).

The brain-based causes of phonological problems remain unknown. One theory is that frequent bouts of ear infections (otitis media) result in enough poor hearing at crucial developmental points to interfere with the child's appreciation of what a set of sounds in a given environment should sound like. Some children with no history of otitis media also have abnormal phonological systems, however. Moreover, they tend to distinguish minimal pairs of words in their production of them, albeit by unconventional means (e.g. using vowel shortening where a final consonant should occur: e.g. /pa/ for "pot" but /pa:/ for "Pa"). Such problems tend to run in families, suggesting a biological basis for the problem, even if actual brain lesions cannot be demonstrated. For such children the problem would seem to lie somewhere in the motor-planning system that converts phonological representations to spoken words.

Another form of SLI is reflected in problems in morphosyntax. In a recent set of studies, Gopnik and her colleagues focus on the hereditary component in this form of specific language impairment. The particular difficulty with morphology reported in this three-generation family is rare, but Gopnik was able to document its existence in a grandmother, in four out of five of her children (all three daughters and one of the two sons), and in eleven of the 24 grandchildren. In these individuals both phonology and morphosyntax are impaired. Indeed, the children are regularly unintelligible up until the age of seven despite normal hearing and intelligence.

In their first set of studies, they noted that dysphasic individuals in this family had particular difficulty with comprehending plurals (e.g. "Show me the books" as compared to "Show me the book") and difficulty making grammaticality judgments on sentences containing errors of number ("the boy eats three cookie"), person ("the boy kiss a pretty girl"), tense ("yesterday the girl pet a dog") and aspect ("the little girl is play with her dog") (Gopnik and Crago, 1991). Argument-structure errors in which, for example, a verb that should take a direct object did not (e.g. "the nice girl gives") were relatively well corrected, by contrast. Production of tense forms was impaired, as was production of plurals for nonsense words. In writing there was a discrepancy between regular and irregular verbs; family members had learned the forms for irregular verbs, but consistently erred on regular verbs, often giving the unmarked form! Problems also were seen with comprehending negative passives, and with derivational morphology.

Similarly with respect to pluralization, the dysphasic subjects had difficulty making plurals on nonsense words like *wug* and *zoop*. One subject whispered "add an s"; another turned *sas* to /sæsIz/ and then added the syllabic plural to all the remaining items (e.g.

/zupIz/). In later analyses, Goad and Rebellati (1994) conducted phonetic analyses of the plural forms that dysphasics in this family produced. In fact the subjects do not assimilate for voicing, that is, they do not mark plurals with a /z/ sound for words that end in voiced consonants, and with a /s/ sound for words that end in unvoiced consonants. This suggests that their pluralization is performed by compounding rather than by a normal rule of affixing.

Particularly striking was comparing the way the dysphasics and their normal siblings took these tests. For the dysphasics the tasks were difficult and time-consuming "as if they were taking a test in a language they did not know particularly well"; for the normals the tasks were quite simple and self-evident.

In a series of papers published in the early 1990s (Matthews, 1994, Gopnik and Crago, 1991; Dalalakis, 1994a and 1994b; Fukuda and Fukuda, 1994; Goad and Gopnik, 1994; Gopnik and Crago, 1994; Gopnik, 1994a, b and c; Kehayia, 1994) Gopnik and her team evaluate more specifically the problems the specific language-impaired members of this family have with pluralization, tense and adjectival inflections in English, and related phenomena in Japanese, Greek, and Inuktitut. They analyze spontaneous discourse, grammaticality judgment tasks, and nonsense-word production tasks. In each instance they are able to ascertain that the language-impaired members of a family, like the unimpaired members, appreciate the meaning that inflectional categories must bear (one vs. more than one, currently or in the past) but are unable to automatically apply the rules. On virtually all these tests of inflectional morphology, the language-impaired subjects performed markedly worse than the unimpaired members of their family, despite normal cognitive abilities generally. On a task to test patients' abilities with grammatical number, for example, they asked subjects to tell whether sentences such as "I drove past several truck on the way home" sound natural or unnatural, or whether subjects were unsure. Rather than automatically applying rules, the subjects have learned rules that they can articulate. However they do not apply them consistently (e.g. when asked how the past tense is produced, one subject said "if it's today, it's *ing*, like *swimming*. 'I went swimming today' and 'yesterday I swamt'") (Matthews, 1994: 133).

While it has been generally understood that specific language impairment tends to run in families, the studies by Gopnik and her colleagues are the first to give such clear-cut indication of genetic predilection for a very specific disorder. Currently there is no information about the brains of the subjects, although apparently they have no history of birth disorders or frank brain damage. However, the specificity of the tasks and analyses Gopnik and her team have employed raises the distinct possibility that biology determines the specific ways that cellular arrangements and connections in the brain can facilitate morphosyntactic aspects of language processing and production.

Numerous explanatory hypotheses have been generated to explain the language disorders of specific language impairment. Some have argued that the problems with inflectional morphology are a secondary by-product of perceptual problems, either in terms of articulation or phoneme perception. Gopnik and her colleagues are able to demonstrate that their subjects perform like normals on the phoneme perception task and generate markedly more errors in speech production on inflectional affixes than on the same structures when they do not function as inflectional affixes. They maintain, rather, that because the language learning of SLI children is delayed, their brains' abilities to acquire morphosyntactic rules for automatic production are dysfunctional. Thus only explicit knowledge of the rules can be applied, resulting in subtle, and sometimes not so subtle, errors (Paradis and Gopnik, 1994).

Conclusion

Study of children with developmental language disorders is of great importance to help those whose brain damage requires remediation. Such cases are also useful for determining the psychological reality of the various aspects of language that can be impaired in such children while others are spared, such as phonological processing. However, they are hard to evaluate in terms of brain regions involved because the nature of the brain malfunction is rarely, if ever, clear. By contrast, the study of childhood aphasia contributes indications of the specific, especially syntactic, abilities that the left hemisphere is particularly good at. At the same time the similarity of all aphasias in children suggests that language abilities are more diffusely organized, at least within the language area, in children than in adults.

7 Right-brain damage

In this chapter, we will consider possible contributions of the right hemisphere to language perception, production and use. Data presented in the aphasia chapters have suggested that the left hemisphere is solely responsible for language. Only in the chapter on language disorders in children was the possibility raised that the right hemisphere *can* participate in language acquisition, in cases of early left-brain damage.

Right-hemisphere lesions do not typically result in any of the classic patterns of language loss. In fact the scarcity of patients with linguistic deficits following right-hemisphere injury was one of the pieces of evidence for lateralization of language in the left hemisphere for most of the population. The right hemisphere has been thought to have little or no language ability except in the case of extensive early left-hemisphere damage. Rather, the right hemisphere has been connected with processing emotions, visuo-spatial materials, music, and the like.

One logical possibility is that the right hemisphere has nearly the same potential for language acquisition as the left but, for efficiency, yields to the left hemisphere. If it were simply more efficient to have one hemisphere take responsibility for language, however, we would expect a random distribution of language in the hemispheres. That is, about half of humans would have the right hemisphere dominant for language, and half would have the left hemisphere dominant. Indeed, this seems to be the case for other animals like mice (if we look at pawedness, of course, not language, as the measure of lateral dominance). It could also be the case that the right hemisphere does acquire some linguistic ability which is then suppressed by the dominant left hemisphere. More likely, it is currently thought, the right hemisphere and the left hemisphere have different patterns of cellular interconnection. These patterns differ so that the standard, left-hemisphere patterns are most appropriate for the analytic abilities needed for language, and perhaps for their later automatization as well, but the right-hemisphere systems, particularly good for holistic sorts of knowledge, can, in a pinch, take on language processing abilities as well. Evidence bearing on this question comes from a number of different populations which we will consider in turn.

Hemispherectomy

In the previous chapter we mentioned the small number of children with a neurological disorder known as Sterge-Weber-Dmitri syndrome, which includes problems with the blood supply to the cortex. The best possible results for these children are achieved by early removal of the entire affected hemisphere. Recall that the remaining hemisphere is able to assume much of the function of the removed hemisphere. Whether the left or the right hemisphere is removed, the children do acquire language. Children who have had their right hemisphere removed are linguistically indistinguishable from children who have intact brains. However, children who have had their left hemisphere removed evidence subtle linguistic difficulties.

Studies of these children with early hemispherectomy, we conclude, cast doubt on *total* equipotentiality of the hemispheres. They also establish considerable right-hemisphere ability to assume language function.

Linguistic abilities in right-brain-damaged adults

The right-brain-damaged patient

Unlike left-brain-damaged patients, who appear in their person to be very similar to who they were before the brain damage, right-brain-damaged patients are perceived as being somehow different. They no longer care for themselves or their dress as carefully as they may have before the brain damage. Their face and their prosody convey what is called "flat affect," as if they were not engaged in a conversation, and their behavior is often quite inappropriate. They may joke about some of the topics we do not generally discuss in our society (such as sex) inappropriately, or interrupt meetings or serious conversations with unrelated comments on things that have distracted them. When they themselves are talking, they may stray off on unimportant tangents and forget to return to the topic at hand. Thus, while their linguistic abilities per se are not markedly impaired, as they are so noticeably in aphasic patients, there are a number of language and communication deficits that they display, which, in turn, yield information about the way the right hemisphere participates in language and communication.

Tone and prosody

The possibility of right-hemisphere contributions to normal language processing and production needs to be considered at a number of different levels. We will start with phonology – the sound system – and then turn to levels of lexical representation, syntax, and text production or pragmatic levels. The phonology of all natural languages contains some prosodic component. For example, all languages use prosody to distinguish questions from assertions. In addition, some languages, like Chinese and Vietnamese, use tone as a suprasegmental distinctive feature (that is, it can distinguish between two words that otherwise sound exactly alike). So, for example, in Toisanese Chinese, the word /hau/ spoken with a high flat pitch means "mouth" while the same string of sounds spoken with a falling pitch started at a mid-level point means the relative location "behind." Since the right hemisphere is dominant for the perception of musical tone, might it also be essential in the production/perception of linguistic tone and/or prosody?

Some researchers have thought that the tone in tone languages might be processed predominantly by the right hemisphere. However, Van Lancker & Fromkin's 1973 dichotic-listening study indicated this was *not* true for normal subjects. Apparently because tone systems serve linguistic functions, discriminating among words that are otherwise pronounced the same, left-hemisphere dominance was shown among Thai speakers. A recent set of studies of aphasic Thai and Chinese speakers provides converging evidence that the left hemisphere is responsible for tone, as tone production (Gandour et al., 1992; Eng Huie, 1994) and perception (Eng Huie, 1994) are impaired in left-hemisphere-damaged aphasics.

However, even in non-tone languages such as English, stress and intonation play a role in the grammar of the language. Standard aspects of linguistic intonation that serve syntactic function (say, to distinguish questions from assertions in many languages) appear to be dominated by the right hemisphere, researchers such as Blumstein and her colleagues (e.g. Blumstein and Cooper, 1974) have demonstrated. Similarly, the perception and production of emotional non-grammatical prosody (say, to convey anger or enthusiasm) is certainly essential for normal participation in everyday discourse. In dichotic-listening tasks, there is a left-ear advantage, suggesting right-hemisphere dominance, for affectively intoned material as well. Subjects are more accurate in judging whether two emotionally intoned sentences are the same or different when the sentences are presented to the left ear. They are also quicker and more accurate in naming the affect presented in the stimulus.

Lexicon

It is generally understood that the words of our internal lexicons are represented primarily in the left hemisphere. However, work with split-brain patients has suggested that there is some lexical knowledge in the right hemisphere of the split-brain patient as well. If a written word is directed to the right hemisphere of such a patient, by presenting it in the left visual field (see Figure 2.8) and preventing the subjects from turning their heads so that it can be seen via the right visual field, the patient will not be able to say the word aloud. However, particularly with concrete and imageable words, such patients will be able to point (with the left hand, of course, but not the right) to a picture of what the word represents, even when they may actually speak saying they have no idea!

Joanette (1994) reports on a comparison of the lexico-semantic production of right-brain-damaged patients and normal controls. In a test of verbal fluency, subjects were asked to name as many words as possible within a two minute time limit. There were four conditions for this production task. In two of the conditions, each of the words had to begin with the same letter. This tested the patients' ability to access vocabulary based on the *form* of the word. In the other conditions, the words needed to be associated with the same *semantic* category (e.g. animals, furniture). The right-brain-damaged subjects performed very similarly to the normal subjects in the conditions based on form. They were also quite similar for the first thirty seconds of the semantic condition. However after the first thirty seconds, the right-brain-damaged subjects produced significantly fewer responses than the normals. This impairment implies that there is some right-hemisphere contribution to the lexical access process for meaning but not for form.

A study by Bloom et al. (1990) demonstrated that right-brain-damaged patients had some difficulty with lexical selection in story-telling contexts, consistently choosing words of less emotional intensity than did their left- brain-damaged or normal control counterparts. They were, in general, less successful in using words to convey emotion.

Syntax

Right-brain-damaged patients also seem to have less flexibility than normals in assigning structural properties to sentences (Schneiderman and Saddy, 1988). For example, in order to appreciate the ambiguity of a sentence such as *The boy hit the man with the cane*, it is necessary to see both the possibilities: "with the cane" can be an adjective phrase describing the man or an instrumental phrase modifying the way in which the boy hit the man. The patients tested by Schneiderman and Saddy could not identify both possibilities.

Emotion in discourse

At the level of text production and language use, the most compelling evidence for right-hemisphere involvement is in the area of emotional aspects of discourse. As we mentioned above, the right hemisphere is dominant for processing emotional prosody. Facial expression of emotion is also controlled predominantly by the right hemisphere, as is appreciation of emotional, facial expressions. Yet when Blonder, Bowers, and Heilman (1991) asked their left-brain-damaged, right-brain-damaged, and normal control subjects to perform a number of tasks designed to distinguish among prosodic, facial and lexical indications of emotion, their right-brain-damaged subjects were able to infer the emotional content of sentences describing emotional situations. This was true for sentences in which the emotional content was signalled directly (e.g. "You were delighted by the bonus") as well as for more difficult "connotative" (e.g. "It was the third anniversary of the death of your child") or "interpretive" (e.g. "After you drink the water, you see the sign") sentences. This speaks against a general disruption in the ability to appreciate emotional situations in patients with right-brain damage.

The Blonder et al. study confirmed previous research on right-brain-damaged patients' difficulty in distinguishing faces and facial expressions. However, their right-brain-damaged subjects also had significantly more difficulty than either the normal control or left-brain-damaged subjects in interpreting *verbal* descriptions of emotional expressions such as "He scowled" or emotional prosody (e.g. "He spoke quickly and breathlessly"). This suggests an actual disruption in the representation of non-verbal (gestural and prosodic) emotional expressions.

Discourse appropriateness

In addition to lexical access and the representation of non-verbal communicative gestures as well as the verbal expression of emotion, a role for the right hemisphere in the organization of discourse has been suggested. To demonstrate the difference between well-formedness at the sentence level and at the discourse level, it is only necessary to examine the difference in status between two strings depending on the context. As sentences, it is clear that *Butter is yellow.* is well-formed and **From work.* is ill-formed. However, in the context of a discourse such as the following, clearly the judgments are reversed:

> Speaker A: I'm surprised to see you at this bus stop. Where are you coming from?
> Speaker B: From work./*Butter is yellow.

Speakers of any language have certain expectations with respect to the organization of both texts (written or oral) and conversations. Learning to produce well-formed discourse is an unconscious process, just as native speakers of a language are not consciously aware of the grammar of their language and learn grammatical rules without explicit instruction. Although the criteria for well-formed discourse may vary slightly from culture to culture, there are a number of pragmatic features of discourse that tend to be observed universally. These expectations were described by the philosopher Paul Grice (1975) as a basic principle of cooperation covering four major conversational "maxims":

(1) *Maxim of Quantity*   In a communicative exchange, participants should not provide too much or too little information.
     Where are you coming from?
     *Somewhere./*I'm coming from West 34th street and Broadway. I walked east for two blocks, crossed the street after waiting for the light and then walked one block north.
(2) *Maxim of Relevance*   Participants should maintain a topic from one utterance to the next, with topic shifts allowed only at certain junctures. This is the maxim violated in the "Butter is yellow" example above.
(3) *Maxim of Manner*   Information should be presented in an organized and clear manner.

> *My hometown has five shopping malls. It is the county seat. My father and mother were both born there. My hometown is a midwestern town of 105,000 inhabitants situated at the center of the Corn Belt. I was brought up there until I was thirteen years old. (Example taken from Finegan & Besnier, 1989)

(4) *Maxim of Quality* In general, people should say and write only things they believe to be true.

Although the fourth maxim clearly has more to do with the content of discourse and other areas of cognition, the first three have an impact on the structure of discourse. Other authors have expanded on Grice's original conversational maxims to capture further generalizations about our unconscious expectations for language use. For example, participants in a discourse must choose and maintain an appropriate level of formality depending on the context. This makes "lexical selection" an important feature of discourse construction; words must be selected to fit the text (*Bye-bye Your Highness; see you!).

Similarly, appropriate phonological and syntactic features must be used. For example, one common feature of casual spoken English is the pronunciation [n] for the ending -ing as in:

I love to go swimmin' and fishin'.

However, in the context of a formal sentence, such casual pronunciations are inappropriate:

*I've been hypothesizin' about nuclear fusion.

Conversely, the use of formal features can be inappropriate in certain contexts. For example, the use of the passive construction would not be appropriate for highly marked, caretaker speech:

*Come on sweetie, all your nice soupy-woupy must be eaten now!

Studies of the discourse produced by right-brain-damaged patients reveal subtle deficits in some of these verbal pragmatic aspects. Bloom et al. (1992) examined the performance of right-brain-damaged patients, left-brain-damaged patients and normal controls on a story-telling task using pictures designed to elicit emotional or non-emotional discourse. The subjects were shown cartoon drawings created for this study, some of which involved an emotional event (such as a girl losing her dog and seeing him run over), and others of which involved a non-emotional event (such as how to fry an egg). In this study, the focus was on the amount of information given. Both left-brain-damaged and right-brain-damaged patients showed some difficulty in producing appropriate amounts of information in their discourse. This is to be expected for the aphasic left-brain-damaged patients. However, the right-brain-damaged group, while producing similar amounts of discourse to that of the normal controls, still failed to produce appropriate amounts of information. In the emotional story context, the performance of the right-brain-damaged patients was particularly impaired. That is, their speech had markedly less content than that of the normals.

One explanation for a set of the conversational problems that right-brain-damaged patients have is that they have impaired abilities to think about what is in the mind of the people they are talking to. This theory, the Theory of Mind, is built on the notion that children after a certain age develop a sensitivity to what their interlocutors know and what they do not. For example, around this time, the children start more appropriately using pronouns in instances when their interlocutor can know who is being referred to, and using proper nouns otherwise. For example, if I'm talking about two women, Henrietta and Jocelyn, I can't refer to first one and then the other in a sentence using only pronouns; "then she hit her on the head" can't be fully interpreted unless we know which pronoun refers to which person. Right-brain-damaged patients will have more difficulty than normals in seeing that referents are made clear. Also, starting in childhood, and extending through our work-lives, we learn how to choose the register of language we use so as to appropriately attend to the differences in power between, say, a boss and an employee. While normals are able to appreciate that one doesn't say "don't do that" to one's boss, right-brain-damaged patients might choose that response as often as "do you think it's possible for us not to do that?" when a similar situation is described (e.g. the boss has just planned a picnic on the day that a surprise party has been planned for her).

Not only do right-brain-damaged patients have difficulties in descriptive discourse and in conversation, generally; they also have difficulties with non-literal language. In a series of studies, Gardner and Brownell and their colleagues have tested right-brain-damaged patients' abilities to appreciate sarcasm and humor, as well as metaphoric meanings of words. (See Brownell et al., 1994, for a review of these studies.) The right-brain-damaged patients characteristically interpret expressions that are intended to be taken non-literally quite literally; by contrast, left-brain-damaged patients, even if they cannot comprehend all the words, can distinguish the two when given the appropriate contextual situations for interpretation. They looked at right-brain-damaged patients' ability to deal with metaphor and idioms and other examples of individual words that have more than one meaning (e.g. *blue*, the color and *blue* meaning sad). Right-brain-damaged patients again often select the literal meanings on these tasks, although under certain conditions the researchers have demonstrated that the patients do have access to the second, more abstract meanings of the words or phrases.

Accessing the abstract meanings of words can be demonstrated by giving the subjects a priming task. Because our mental dictionary is organized along semantic lines (as well as phonological, morphological, and orthographic ones), processing a word from a given semantic category gets the subject to the right "area" of the lexicon, making reactions to subsequent words in that same semantic area quicker. This quickening of reaction times is referred to as "priming." In such a task subjects must make some decision about the second word they see in a pair. For example, subjects may have to decide whether the word "blue" is a word. The first word is either related to it (e.g. *sad*) or not (e.g. *dog*). In the specific studies we are talking about here, the meaning of the first priming word crucially relates to the non-literal meaning of the second word or phrase. On such tasks, we see that the response time for the brain-damaged subjects to decide that the second word is a real word in English, or the idiom is a real idiom in English, is facilitated for the right-brain-damaged patients just as it is for normals and left-brain-damaged patients, indicating that the non-literal meanings of the second word in each pair are available to them. It seems one must conclude, then, as Brownell and colleagues (1994) do, that the problem lies not with the knowledge of non-literal features of language, but rather in applying that knowledge in the processing involved for performing such tasks.

Split-brain patients

Given that the right hemisphere is capable of acquiring language when the left hemisphere is removed or severely damaged, it is logical to consider the possibility that the right hemisphere has some linguistic abilities not normally in evidence due to the inhibitory effects of the dominant left hemisphere. In split-brain patients, the reader will recall, this interhemispheric communication is interrupted. Thus stimuli presented to the left visual field cannot be fully processed linguistically. The right hemisphere registers such stimuli, and may even react to them, however. In some studies (e.g. Zaidel and Peters, 1981) some split-brain patients have been able to extract linguistic information from stimuli presented to the right hemisphere. Some, for example, could pick a rhyming word from a list of choices. However, even for the majority of split-brain patients whose right hemispheres do demonstrate some rudimentary linguistic abilities, the isolated right hemisphere cannot comment on its perceptions.

In a review of studies of commissurotomy patients, Gazzaniga (1983) provides a description of the right-hemisphere linguistic abilities of the two (out of the 44 patients living in 1982) split-brain patients who had developed right-hemisphere speech (presumably after the surgery). For both of these patients, comprehension of stimuli presented to the right hemisphere was essentially normal. Both were able to name objects, carry out verbal commands and even detect semantic peculiarities in sentences presented to the right hemisphere alone.

However, the left hemisphere in both patients remained the "more talkative," dominant hemisphere. This can be seen in the response of the patient P.S. to bilateral presentation of a brief story. The patient was presented a series of five slides each of which flashed one word into the right visual field (left hemisphere) and one word into the left visual field (right hemisphere). In normals, the information from each half of the slide is integrated and the story reads as follows:

MARY + ANN   MAY + COME   VISIT + INTO   THE + TOWN
SHIP + TODAY

P.S. demonstrated an appreciation of the information presented both to the left and right hemispheres but reported the story quite differently, his left hemisphere at first reporting only what it saw and, only when pressed, did it struggle to integrate the verbal responses of the right hemisphere (Gazzaniga, 1983):

> P.S. Ann come into town today. [NOTE: These were all, and only, processed by the left hemisphere]
>
> E. Anything else?
>
> P.S. On a ship.
>
> E. Who?
>
> P.S. Ma.
>
> E. What else?
>
> P.S. To visit.
>
> E. What else?
>
> P.S. To see Mary Ann.
>
> E. Now repeat the whole story.
>
> P.S. Ma ought to come into town today to visit Mary Ann on the boat.

Conclusion

In order to reach the conclusion that the right hemisphere normally participates in some way in the perception or production of language, we look for evidence of linguistic deficits following right-brain damage.

We have looked at the abilities of a surgically isolated right hemisphere and at experimental techniques devised for presenting linguistic stimuli only to the right hemisphere. The brains of commissurotomy patients are certainly not representative of the general population given the history of seizures. Yet, these commissurotomy studies, along with dichotic and tachistoscopic presentation studies, do provide evidence that the normal, adult, right hemisphere can, under special circumstances, demonstrate linguistic ability.

While the right hemisphere does not appear to have much responsibility in normal individuals for core linguistic processes such as phonology, morphology, and syntax, it contributes importantly to a set of paralinguistic phenomena. Intonation appears to be dealt with by the right hemisphere, whether it indicates syntactic structure or emotional communication. Some aspects of lexical selection appear to have substantial right-hemisphere involvement, like the ability to appreciate multiple meanings, especially non-literal ones, of words. Moreover, a host of pragmatic abilities appear to be impaired with right-hemisphere (but not left-hemisphere) damage. These include the abilities to appreciate humor, sarcasm, implication, discourse appropriateness, the interlocutor's knowledge, and the like.

8 Dementia

The term "dementia" is very broad. It refers to the results of a number of different diseases all of which lead to a loss of intellectual abilities. After we consider the relation between language and cognition, we will turn to the usual course of some types of dementia and their effect on the language of the dementing person. Dementia is caused by the deterioration of brain tissue. Different dementias affect different parts of the brain, but they do not result in obvious brain damage in distinctly localized areas of the brain the way aphasias do. Rather they appear as more generalized atrophy.

One crucial distinction for our purposes is the distinction between cortical and subcortical dementias. In the cortical dementias, the cellular changes associated with dementia are primarily in cortical areas; in the subcortical ones, conversely, the cellular changes are primarily in subcortical structures. The most commonly known cortical dementia is Alzheimer's disease. In this disease, the characteristic changes in cortical cells result in patients showing at least three of the following four symptoms: they evidence problems with language; they have memory problems; they have problems performing new tasks with knowledge they already know (e.g. spelling "world" backwards); and they have personality changes. Many patients become markedly more irritable, even belligerent; there is one instance where an adult daughter complained that her mother, who had previously been wonderfully critical, had become uninterestingly "nice" with Alzheimer's dementia.

The most common subcortical dementia occurs in perhaps

one-third of cases of Parkinson's disease. The difficulties in walking and in speech are remarkably similar. Patients may have trouble initiating each, and move quite slowly, at least at the beginning, however, they may speed up and, in walking, stumble. Speaking, their speech may end up muttered unintelligibly. The language changes in Parkinson's disease are more subtle as we discuss below.

Language and cognition

The language of dementing patients presents a unique opportunity for examining the relationship between language and cognition. The pattern of dissociation of abilities in dementia can yield information regarding the normal relationship – dependence or independence – between language and more general cognitive abilities. A patient with Alzheimer's dementia once told one of us that the woman in the Cookie Theft Picture (see Figure 4.1) was in a "turmoil of smin." Was he simply unable to say that the woman should have been upset because so many things were going wrong in her kitchen, or was he unable to figure out from the picture that indeed she was not upset, as most normal patients report? To study language production and comprehension abilities in dementing patients is to explore the boundaries between syntax and semantics and among semantics, real world knowledge, and reasoning abilities.

Wernicke himself was concerned about how thought and cognition related in his famous 1874 paper in which he distinguished Wernicke's aphasia from Broca's aphasia and predicted conduction aphasia. In fact, one of the two patients he asserted had Wernicke's aphasia was, our current analysis strongly suggests, a patient with dementia (Mathews et al., 1994). Because patients with both Wernicke's aphasia and Alzheimer's dementia include empty words (e.g. "this," "the thing") and nonsense phrases in their speech, it is hard to determine if there is underlying knowledge beneath what they say. To distinguish whether one is seeing the language changes of Wernicke's aphasia or the language-plus-cognitive changes of Alzheimer's dementia, it is not sufficient to rely on patients' language problems; we must consider whether there is a history of a more generalized cognitive and behavioral decline. If so, we say that we are looking at Alzheimer's dementia, and that the language reflects both cognitive and linguistic impairments. If there was a sudden onset of language problems with no history of memory or other cognitive problems, we assume we are seeing Wernicke's aphasia.

Subcortical dementias

Most frequently seen among the subcortical dementias is Parkinson's disease which affects mostly subcortical brain areas. This kind of brain tissue deterioration has significant impact on the patient's ability to produce speech. Not only do patients with Parkinson's disease start walking slowly and with difficulty, and move slowly generally, this slow and halting behavior extends to control of the vocal apparatus. Parallel to the dysarthria or difficulty in articulating speech sounds seen in these patients, there is often a dysgraphia or disturbance in the ability to write. For example, writing samples exhibit both micrographia or a tendency to write very small letters, and an inappropriate use of space in writing. Of course, either of these symptoms might be attributed to loss of muscle control without any damage to brain representation for language.

Though these movement symptoms are the most striking for patients with Parkinson's disease, there are also cognitive changes in the one-third of patients with Parkinson's disease who also have dementia. This dementia consists primarily of memory problems and problems operating on the knowledge they already have. Moreover, a closer examination of the linguistic output of patients with subcortical dementia has revealed subtle effects on language itself. Consider the following example from a Parkinsonian patient's written description of the BDAE Cookie Theft Picture taken from Obler (1983; underlining added):

> the boy on the stoll tripp_ and the girl laugh_ at the boy and then she spill_ water on the floor.

Of the four underlined omissions or substitutions of letters, three involve morphological word-endings. This tendency to err more frequently on inflectional endings is common in dementing patients. It cannot be explained by simple inattention. While it is true that the ability to pay attention to a task is impaired in the dementias and distraction is common, such problems in writing should distribute themselves randomly across words if attention or the ability to self-monitor were the only explanation of the writing problems. Here instead, it is the linguistic properties of words that appear to render inflectional endings particularly vulnerable to error. Murray Grossman and his colleagues (Grossman et al., 1994) have demonstrated additional lexical problems in patients with Parkinson's disease. When exposed to a new verb (*wamble*, meaning "to return home") and asked about it 10 minutes later, some patients learned nothing about the verb, while others picked up only semantic information but not information about syntactic use.

Further examples of linguistic disturbance in subcortical dementia are found in lexical-selection errors. Consider the following example from Dr.T., a patient with a subcortical dementing disease called *progressive supranuclear palsy* (a neurological disorder resulting in bodily rigidity as well as dysarthria – muscular problems at the end-stage of speech production – and dementia) whose language is reported more fully in Obler et al., 1980. In describing the Cookie Theft Picture, he writes:

> The young lady he is hang up in mischief.

Not only does he omit the affix "ing," he presumably intends "hanging up in" for "involves." In addition to such lexical and morphological disturbances, Grossman and his colleagues have demonstrated sentence-processing problems in patients with Parkinson's disease. They attribute these problems to memory and to attentional deficits resulting from poor distribution of dopamine to areas of the frontal lobe that are involved in cortical networks for sentence comprehension (e.g. Grossman et al., 1992).

Cortical dementias

In the *cortical* dementias, especially Alzheimer's disease, patients have symptoms much more like those of the aphasias. This is not surprising since the cellular damage to the brain, while widespread, is primarily in the temporal and frontal lobes of patients with the disease. Consider the following speech sample from a patient with advanced Alzheimer's dementia cited by Bayles & Kaszniak, 1987:

> "No, for goodness sake. What is you doing? Coming home from a story, or playing? My parents is a has a present for you .. Ah, your parents has the house-cleaning, Timmy. We, we, no. Running out at three, then, the car wash, they, uh, fill, four, happy everyone, then can come back again."

In terms of context, this discourse is clearly lacking in cohesion, with over-frequent topic shifts. It is also repetitive and fairly empty, reminiscent of the speech of a Wernicke's aphasic. In addition, there are frequent morphological and syntactic errors as well as lexical selection errors. The words *story* and *is* are misselected. In the case of "is," the patient repairs his error in selecting a verb for the sentence, but does not correct the form of the verb (i.e., my parents (pl.) is/has (sing.)). This difficulty with number agreement is seen again in "What *is you* doing?" and "Your *parents has* . . ." In addition, two sentence fragments are lacking subjects: "Running out . . ." and "can come back again." Only word order is relatively well preserved. One of the interesting questions is, then, is this patient's grammar affected by his dementing illness? Or is an intact grammar unable to function burdened by loss of memory, inattention and lack of self-monitoring? To begin to answer these questions, a closer look at some individual cases and specific linguistic deficits is necessary.

The lexicon

Patients begin to experience word-finding difficulty early in dementing illnesses. It is normal to have transient problems in finding words from the mental lexicon, of course. Everyone has experienced the "tip of the tongue" feeling that comes when the name for something once known cannot be retrieved. Both experiential and experimental evidence suggest that the representation of the missing word has not been erased from our mental dictionary. The most usual case is for the "missing" word to reappear after a time, without outside help. Often, even during the time in which the word cannot be recalled, some information about the word is available. The number of syllables, some sound(s) or letter(s) or the stress pattern of the word may be recalled. Of course this partial information is not always completely accurate.

Picture a faculty member attempting to remember the name of a student. She says ". . . five letters, two vowels, three consonants – alternating." The name turns out to be "Morris." In this case the "mistake" in recollection might be explained by an appeal to a phonological (one [r] sound) rather than orthographic (two "r" letters) memory. Our partial recall of words we temporarily cannot access is not always even this accurate. However, the very phenomenon of remembering some information about "missing" words and eventually recalling them without re-learning them suggests that access to lexical representation is at issue and not the representation itself. Interestingly, aphasics can often tell information about words that they cannot recall, as can normal individuals, including elderly individuals after the age of seventy who have more trouble remembering the names of things than younger ones. However, with patients with dementia it is hard to get them to engage in this task, so we cannot use tip-of-the-tongue data to be sure whether their problem is with accessing the words or with loss of the actual words themselves. One way to judge which of these two is the case is to see if a given word consistently provides problems across modalities (for example, in using the writing system as well as the auditory system). There is still controversy in the field as to the extent to which patients with Alzheimer's disease exhibit a consistent loss of lexical items.

Another way to look at this issue is to determine when the inability to name things may even extend to common objects in some dementing patients such as WLP, the patient with Alzheimer's disease described in Schwartz et al. (1979). Although she was unable to name even five percent of common objects presented to her in pictures relatively early in her dementing illness, she was seventy percent accurate in choosing the correct answer from among several multiple-choice options. Multiple-choice naming tests are also designed in such a way that the pattern of *wrong* choices a person makes also provides information about their knowledge of words. For example, given a picture of a fork, the multiple-choice answers might be:

(a) pork (similar in sound and spelling)
(b) knife (related in meaning)
(c) lamp (unrelated)
(d) fork (correct)

On ninety percent of the test items for which WLP did not choose the correct answer, she chose the semantically related item. This suggests that the picture was meaningful for her in spite of the fact that she could not consistently choose the correct lexical item: a question of difficulty in *access* rather than lost representation.

Later on in the course of her illness, WLP made even more naming errors. She also chose fewer semantically related words and more unrelated words. Her performance on picture-matching tasks began to evidence some breakdown in semantic categorization.

Research with normals has shown that semantically related words are linked to each other in the mental lexicon. Hearing one word in a semantic area (e.g. *nurse*) makes a person quicker in making judgments about the status of related words (e.g. *doctor*). WLP's choice of semantically related words on the picture-naming task demonstrates that in the early stages of her illness, these connections in the lexicon were still present and available to her for completing the naming task. As WLP's dementia progressed, however, her organization of semantic fields became impaired. Given pictures of dogs, cats and birds to associate with the labels "dog," "cat," and "bird," WLP frequently labeled pictures of cats "dog." She very rarely made this mistake with pictures of birds. Her sub-grouping of animals was principled but non-standard. This impairment extended beyond the purely linguistic level. When asked to match pictures of various dogs or cats to pictures of a typical dog, WLP always chose the cat.

Syntax and paragrammatism

Not only the lexicon is affected in Alzheimer's dementia. That other aspects of the grammar are not entirely spared is demonstrated by the uneven effects of dementing illness on different aspects of speech production. If inattention were the sole cause of speech errors in dementing patients, as we said above, the distribution of the errors should not be skewed toward any grammatical category.

In the speech of LB, a dementing patient whose speech is described in Obler (1983), paragrammatic errors, that is, errors which evidence disturbed grammatical representation, or, at least, production processes, do occur regularly. Some errors, such as omissions, affect all parts of speech equally. When LB intended to refer to the name of the guy next door, he said "The guy next name," clearly a case of omission for "the guy next door's name." (Obler, 1983: 276.) However, other kinds of substitution errors and errors where the patient repeats an item said previously, now inappropriately (called perseverative errors), tend to occur more frequently with inflectional endings, suggesting some disturbance in the grammar itself.

Consider the following example of LB describing a war experience in which he perseverates in the past-tense form when he uses the word *lined.*

> Whenever they felt like it they would flip uh out machine guns and set them out and tell 'ems, us to *lined* up just to scare the devil[3] but we didn't know when they were going to pull them.

One famous example of a dementing person with an extreme dissociation between the functioning of formal grammar and the ability to produce meaningful utterances is described in Whitaker (1976). Her patient, HCEM, was a 59 year old woman who suffered from presenile dementia, a term used at that time for likely Alzheimer's disease starting before age 65. She had little or no spontaneous speech. She could not name even common objects nor accurately read numbers. Her speech during examinations was largely echolalic, that is, she repeated the examiner's utterances. However, many aspects of her language behavior in testing situations seemed to indicate a relatively intact grammar. If the examiner began a familiar song, HCEM would finish it. The examiner spoke a version of English strongly influenced by British English, yet HCEM's repetitions were all in her own American dialect.

Each of these behaviors is compatible with two possibilities: it may be that HCEM's grammar is intact and it guided her production of the utterances, or it may be that she has, like all of us, a separate store of over-learned material and that is how she was able to complete the song. However, HCEM would also correct intentionally deviant utterances. She would make phonological corrections if the named object was in her field of vision. For example, with a dollar bill on the table, the examiner (HW) would say "tollar bill" and HCEM would say "dollar bill." If the object was not present, HCEM reproduced the phrase with the phonemic "error." Perhaps most interestingly, HCEM corrected grammatically incorrect sentences in her repetitions. If HW said "I have hair gray," HCEM repeated "I have gray hair." She also corrected word order in major constituents, person and number agreement and tense usage. When reading morphologically complex words, she often read another complex word with the same root (e.g. *intuitive* for *intuition*). In short, she showed signs of having some phonological and semantic representation for words as well as some sensitivity to syntactic features of sentences. Whitaker referred to this case as an example of isolation of the language function. HCEM's grammar survived the damage to her brain but lost its ability to interface with other cognitive systems.

Spared language abilities

Interestingly, automatic aspects of language are spared until quite late in Alzheimer's disease. For a long time it was thought that patients remain able to read aloud with no difficulties. Recently Patterson and her colleagues (1994) report that irregularly spelled low frequency words (such as *yacht*) do pose problems for these patients. Nevertheless in the early and even middle stages the ability for patients to read aloud, when they make so many naming errors and have empty speech, is quite impressive.

The other automatic language abilities that remain with them quite late are the ability to appropriately produce phonology (although they make speech errors that often go uncorrected, (McNamara et al., 1992), unlike normal elderly who make markedly more speech errors than young, but correct them equally often to young normals), and surface syntax (although as we said, para-grammatisms may occur). The patient who reported that the woman in the Cookie Theft Picture was in a turmoil of smin, also pointed out that "it's quite torrential here, although not torrential here," locating a low-frequency lexical item to describe the over-flowing water, and using the relatively low-frequency functor "al-though." Indeed, this choice of low-frequency functors, even if they are not used semantically correctly, appears to distinguish patients with Alzheimer's disease from those with Wernicke's aphasia who manage to avoid them, choosing the logically simpler functors *and*, *or*, and *but* to phrase their correctly structured sentences.

Some pragmatic abilities, however, are spared until quite late in these patients. Thus in the early stages, when patients are unable to remember things or remember the names of things, they will comment on this, perhaps with a self-deprecating chuckle. In the middle stages, even when the patients are producing quite nonsen-sical discourse in large amounts, the firm examiner can interrupt them. One patient kept noting to one of us (LKO) that I was so "normal," suggesting, although he exhibited little distress, that he had some awareness of his problems. Eye contact is still quite well preserved until late stages, as is the ability to appropriately be quiet in conversation when the examiner interrupts one firmly, and then to speak, whether the speech is related or not, when the examiner has asked a question, or otherwise indicated it is time for the patient's conversational turn.

Conversation and other pragmatic abilities

In the chapter on right-brain damage, we discussed some of the principles involved in constructing appropriate discourse. In the course of dementing illness, patients are likely to develop difficul-ties in observing principles of appropriate quantity, relevance, and manner. These inabilities extend to non-verbal communication as well. Bayles, Kaszniak and Tomoeda (1987) studied this phenom-enon in twenty severely demented patients: eighty-five percent of the patients made eye contact appropriately; sixty-four percent answered appropriately when thanked for their time. Half would correct an incorrect statement made deliberately by the examiner, and verbally interrupt the examiner. Nearly half the patients could appropriately shake hands when the examiner stuck out a hand in the traditional gesture. But only a quarter would clarify one of their responses when the examiner requested that they do so, and fewer than one in twenty complimented the examiner after being themselves complimented.

Although not every aspect of conversational ability is equally impaired in these patients, all of the functions studied are significantly impaired. The authors do not discuss the extent of formal linguistic deficits in their patient population and it is important to bear in mind that these kinds of abilities are dissociable.

Hamilton (1994a) has documented the development of conversational breakdown in a patient with Alzheimer's disease over the course of several years. The patient's ability to initiate topics or to keep to Hamilton's topics increased progressively; by the later stages her role in "conversation" was virtually nil.

Subpatterns of decline in Alzheimer's dementia

In recent years, it is becoming clear that there are a number of subpatterns of decline, even within specific syndromes like dementia of the Alzheimer's type. Some patients get markedly more prominent language disturbances in the earlier stages, while others show markedly more predominant non-language decline. Many believe that predominant language disturbance is linked to an earlier onset of Alzheimer's disease. In some rare families in which Alzheimer's disease occurs in fifty percent of the children, onset of language problems may be as early as the mid-thirties or forties, although patients find ways of masking them; one patient LKO tested covered his mouth when speaking so completely that the listener could not be sure if the mumbling made sense or not. By contrast, patients with onset in their eighties are more likely to have substantially spared language abilities as compared to their other cognitive and daily self-care abilities. Why earlier onset should be associated with more severe language problems is unclear. Our focus in this chapter, of course, has been on the sizable group of individuals who do evidence language disturbance.

Comparison of the language disturbances of aphasia and dementia

A comparison of the language problems of particular patients with aphasia and with dementia allows for a comparison of the cognitive versus linguistic decline in each of the two forms of brain damage.

Both aphasic and demented patients produce some speech with disturbed form and some with unusual content. In general, it is the demented population that shows a greater weakening of the ability to encode meanings, the connection between cognition and language.

For example, both Wernicke's aphasics and demented patients experience difficulty with the use of functors. However, as explained in Obler (1983), the typical Wernicke's patient uses only a subset of the functors available in his or her language, with a marked preference for the "emptier" ones such as "and." Demented patients, on the other hand, are more likely to *misuse* a wide range of functors, as can be seen from the following examples from LA (Obler, 1983):

(a)   I'd like a cup of coffee *but* I'd like one.
(b)   The mother's *neither* caring, the son's *neither* caring *or* can't help it.

Stevens (1991) has suggested that this kind of difference in patterns of errors might serve as a diagnostic for differentiating linguistic disturbances in aphasia and SDAT (senile dementia of the Alzheimer's type). On a test battery with many subtests, the clearest differences were found in tasks involving descriptions of actions and the use of objects. SDAT patients were more likely to not respond, respond with something irrelevant, or perseverate on a previous response. Aphasics in this study, although sometimes giving incomplete responses, were more likely to circumlocute or produce phonemic paraphasias (substitutions of one or two phonemes in the word) or neologisms (strings of phonemes that sound like words but cannot be identified with any possible target word in English). The SDAT patients were exhibiting difficulties in communication that, while perhaps involving lexical or grammatical disturbances, surely are centered more in the area of discourse and conversational skills.

Progressive aphasias

We usually think of the linguistic disturbances of aphasia as having a sudden onset and those of dementia, a more gradual onset. There are, however, cases of progressive aphasia brought on by brain disease rather than stroke or injury. Diagnosing such a patient as aphasic rather than demented is difficult because we associate progressive decline with the dementias. However if language is the only area impaired, and the patient continues to perform normally on all other cognitive tasks, the diagnosis must be progressive aphasia. Here we can see similarities as well as points of departure.

One patient with progressive aphasia without dementia is described by Parkin (1993). This patient, TOB, had great difficulty in word finding in certain circumstances. He had difficulty providing definitions of common words. His errors ranged from overly vague ("needle" defined as "more positive application to females") to wrong (for example, he considered "squirrel" to be "a bird that flies"). However, his comprehension was essentially intact. On a test of matching spoken words to pictures, TOB made no errors. He was also quite capable of naming described objects. Occasional instances of non-comprehension occurred mainly with low-frequency words such as "dissertation."

TOB had difficulty in reading words with irregular spelling, often regularizing the pronunciation, and a parallel difficulty in writing/ spelling. Receptively, however, his performance was much better. On a lexical decision task he correctly identified all of the items that were deemed "pseudo-homonyms," that is irregularly spelled words that, when spelled regularly, are in fact not correctly spelled words in English (e.g. *goast*). In sum, the fact that his skills in processing "input" remained spared while those for "output" were impaired permits us to call this an aphasia rather than a dementia. The fact that it got progressively worse is what was surprising since he did not have a tumor. The causes of progressive aphasia remain unknown; only recently has it been distinguished from the cortical dementias.

Distinguishing the language changes of Alzheimer's disease from those of normal aging

In the early period, when the primary naming problem looks like the naming problem of anomic aphasia, it is not only important to distinguish the language changes of Alzheimer's disease from aphasia. It must also be distinguished, at that stage, from the naming problem of normal aging. Some scholars have argued that, indeed, the language changes associated with Alzheimer's disease are simply an exaggeration of what happens with normal aging. Conversational conventions can be broken in both normal adults as well as demented patients. These include the self-centeredness in discourse (which could result from substantial hearing loss that the speaker wants to mask from the listener) and repeating things one has said before, not remembering one has said them before, nor marking them as one is expected to pragmatically with a phrase such as "as I told you before."

Some behaviors, however, are seen in demented patients that are never seen in normals. One of these is the response to phonemic cues on a naming test. Such cues are very helpful in enabling even very old, normal, elderly patients to recover the correct lexical item that they can not remember the name of. Even when they do not help, normal elderly, unlike patients with Alzheimer's disease, will never simply blurt out a word that begins with the sound (a demented patient, by contrast, when given the cue /b/ for the word "beaver" might say *banana*, not recognizing the inappropriateness of such a response). Also, patients with Alzheimer's disease will sometimes blithely produce neologistic terms in their speech (like the example at the beginning of this chapter of the patient whose word "smin" had no obvious target); normal elderly never will.

Bilingual dementia

Although we discuss bilingualism in more detail in chapter 10, it is worth mentioning bilingual dementia here, as there are additional aspects of linguistic competence to be considered. Just as we see that bilingual aphasics might be found to have quite disparate linguistic skills in each of their languages after brain injury, brain disease may have different effects on each of a patient's languages. Much more than in aphasic patients, the most spared language is likely to be the one learned first, even if it is not the language used most before the onset of the disease or the language of the post-onset environment. Table 8.1 from De Santi et al. (1990) provides an example of different linguistic deficits in the two languages of four Yiddish-English bilinguals.

A healthy bilingual has the ability to produce and/or comprehend utterances in more than one language. The healthy bilingual has an internal set of rules governing language choice. In the case of bilinguals who make use of the resources of both languages in conversations with other bilinguals, the languages are not mixed randomly. The choice of switch points is governed by a set of principles discussed in chapter 10. As mentioned above, research on language dissolution in monolingual dementia patients has shown that conversational skills such as knowing when to take one's turn are relatively well preserved in mild stages of dementia whereas other discourse skills, such as appropriately keeping to the topic (topic maintenance; Hamilton, 1994a), and repairing speech errors (Hamilton, 1994b, McNamara et al., 1992) are more severely affected early in the dementing process.

The effects of dementing illness on bilinguals' language-choice pragmatics are quite striking (Hyltenstam and Stroud, 1989). De Santi et al. (1990), for example, report on testing and conversation with the same four bilinguals whose linguistic difficulties are summarized in the table below. Each patient was interviewed in English by a monolingual interviewer and in Yiddish by an interviewer who, although bilingual, used only Yiddish throughout the interviews. Language choice by the demented patients ranged from almost entirely appropriate to almost never appropriate. One patient, patient D, who did have problems in both of his languages, nevertheless always chose the right language for the interviewer. Patient C, the most severely demented of the four, often chose the wrong language in both the Yiddish and English contexts. Patient E sometimes spoke Yiddish with the monolingual English examiner, a more marked error than that of Patient B whose only

Table 8.1. *General language behavior of four bilingual demented subjects*

Language Behavior	Patient B E	Patient B Y	Patient C E	Patient C Y	Patient D E	Patient D Y	Patient E E	Patient E Y
Naming problems	+	n/a	+	+	+	—	+	+
Paraphasic errors	+	—	+	+	+	—	+	+
Neologisms	—	—	+	+	+	—	+	+
Circumlocutions	—	—	+	+	+	+	+	+
Perseveration	+	—	+	+	+	+	+	+
Illogical responses	—	—	+	+	+	—	+	+
Topic loss	—	—	+	+	+	—	+	—

Note: Key: E = English; Y = Yiddish; n/a = not available; + = The problem listed was evidenced in the sessions; — = The problem listed was not evidenced in the sessions.

Source: From De Santi, S., L. K. Obler, H. Sabo-Abramson, J. Goldberger. Discourse abilities and deficits in multilingual dementia, in Joanette, Y. and H. Brownell, eds., *Discourse ability and brain damage*, New York: Springer-Verlag, 1990: 224.

Table 8.2. *Code-switching with bilingual and monolingual
interlocutors*

With bilingual interlocutor

Subject	C-S	+EQ	− EQ	− FM
Patient B	4	4	0	0
Patient C	87	72	15	3
Patient D	24	23	1	0
Patient E	57	50	6	1

With monolingual interlocutor

Subject	C-S	Utter	+ EQ	− FM
Patient B	0	350	0	0
Patient C	68	888	68	0
Patient D	0	944	0	0
Patient E	23	1664	21	0

Note: Key: C-S = Number of code-switches; Utter = number of
utterances; + EQ = number of code-switches that follow the
equivalence constraint; − EQ = number of code-switches that do not
follow the equivalence constraint; − FM = number of code-switches
that do not follow the free morpheme constraint.
Source: From De Santi, S., L. Obler, H. Sabo-Abramson, J. Goldberger,
Discourse abilities and deficits in multilingual dementia, in Joanette,
Y. and H. Brownell, eds., *Discourse ability and brain damage*. New
York: Springer-Verlag, 1990: 224.

"wrong" choice was to speak English in the Yiddish interview
which was conducted by a bilingual.

The subjects in De Santi et al. (1990) also differed in the extent
to which they code-switched during the interviews. Although the
Yiddish interview was intended to be entirely in Yiddish, the
interviewer's bilingualism created an appropriate context for code-
switching and all four subjects did switch to some extent. Two of
the subjects, patients C and E, also inappropriately switched into
Yiddish with the monolingual interviewer.

Examining the code-switches themselves according to the criteria outlined in chapter 10, De Santi et al. found that the vast majority of code-switches were of the linguistic type made by normal bilinguals. These linguistic-rule-governed aspects of bilingual language behavior seem to be more resistant to the effects of dementing illness than are the pragmatic abilities of these patients which are presumably governed by "executive" functions associated with the frontal lobes.

Conclusion

In subcortical dementias, the problems lie most obviously with speech rather than language. However, subtle problems can be seen with naming, lexical selection, list generation, affixal morphology (in writing, at least), and sentence comprehension.

In the cortical dementias, especially those which begin at a relatively young age, language problems are more evident. While phonology, surface-level syntax, and reading aloud are relatively spared, lexicon and semantics are severely impaired. Simple pragmatic abilities, such as responding when a question is asked and keeping eye-contact, are spared until relatively late in the course of the disease, but more complex ones such as inference or monitoring what the other participant in a conversation already knows, disappear. Non-language aspects of cognition (in particular declines in memory, attention, and the ability to manipulate ideas) contribute heavily to the apparent linguistic decline. These are linked to the frontal, parietal, and temporal lobes where cellular changes are most severe. Although language can be impaired independent of thought, as we have seen in the chapters on aphasia, it seems that thought cannot be impaired without impairment in language performance.

9 Disorders of the written word: dyslexia and dysgraphia

From a linguist's perspective, the written language system is clearly secondary to the oral language system. After all, virtually everyone in the world has use of oral (or gestural) language, while not everyone is able to read. Moreover, in the past, even smaller proportions of populations were able to read and write. Indeed, we assume that spoken language developed long before written language in the history of human development. Also, written language depends on oral language but the converse is not true. Thus the linguist may be more interested in focusing on the most basic form of language, oral language.

For the psycholinguist and neurolinguist, however, the additional systems involved in processing written language are of interest in and of themselves. The psycholinguist wants to know how it is that normal humans can read; the neurolinguist is interested in how reading abilities can break down and what patterns of breakdown tell us about the normal reading process. In this chapter we will focus on disorders of the reading system, and then point to their relation to problems with writing and spelling.

Dyslexia: definitions

The term *dyslexic* means at least three different things. It can refer to children who have particular difficulties learning to read. It can also refer to these children when they become adults; even if they can now read they may still manifest some of the problems associated with the reading disorder. It can also refer to people – usually adults – who have already acquired reading and become brain-damaged. In our view, the difficulties of acquiring reading and the consequences of these difficulties are quite different from the reading difficulties that can follow brain damage to areas of the brain that were previously involved in reading. We will call the phenomenon associated with brain damage *alexia* as it is often – but not always! – referred to in the literature.

Childhood dyslexia

In many ways the study of child dyslexics is more difficult than that of adult dyslexics, since in the literate adult we assume that reading was fully developed before the brain damage. In the child, we must first know what the normal processes of reading *acquisition* are, and what non-language cognitive abilities are necessary for reading to be acquired. Only then can we start to develop an understanding of how reading, or aspects of reading, can pose difficulties in acquisition. Frith (1985) proposes a four-stage acquisition process in which each stage builds on the previous one. First the child develops logographic skills, that is, the ability to recognize familiar words in their entirety. Then alphabetic skills are acquired. In this stage the child learns to identify individual phonemes with individual letters (graphemes). In the third stage, orthographic skills are acquired. Here, higher level clusters of letters, ideally corresponding to morphemes, are identified. In the fourth stage, which may not be achieved by all, due to lack of practice in reading or due to neurological factors, ability to read the written language becomes entirely independent of spoken language.

It is certainly true that there are many different sorts of developmental dyslexics. One way of categorizing a number of such children is to note that some have particular difficulties with identifying whole words (Boder [1970] terms these *dyseidetic*) while others have particular difficulty with decoding the sounds associated with letters (Boder calls these the *dysphonetic*). The problems identifying whole words show up in English with irregularly spelled words. A dyseidetic child may see the word "some" and read it phonetically as two syllables /somi/. Children who have difficulty decoding sounds may learn words as "sight words" but any time they see a new word, e.g. many proper names, they will slow down and make errors. One such child read the name Travis as /tarvs/ throughout a book.

According to Frith's scheme, if a child has difficulty with any particular stage, he or she may develop compensatory strategies, but will in fact have problems with any sort of reading at the later stages. Even if this child is able eventually to pass for a normal reader, neurolinguistic tests designed to tease out problems with reading will be able to demonstrate that these children (or the adults they become) do not read with the full flexibility that normal readers have.

Another way of looking at the difficulties children may show when acquiring reading considers the low-level cognitive abilities that must underlie reading. Tallal (1980) for example, has noted that a certain percentage of child dyslexics have difficulties on tasks requiring quick processing of auditory sounds. She hypothesizes that the basic problems, at least for these dyslexics, arise as a consequence of difficulties with sequencing sounds in time.

Another controversy in the field is the question of whether some minimal IQ is required in order to learn to read. One interesting group of what used to be called "idiots savants" are called *hyperlexics.* These are children who apparently teach themselves to read at a very early age, and can read words aloud – even those that are irregularly spelled – with great facility, despite the fact that there is no evidence that they comprehend what they are reading. Interestingly, these children invariably suffer from autism, a disorder (whose neurological cause is unknown) that most severely affects a person's ability to interact with others. From infancy these children are unhappy being cuddled, and as they develop they never acquire good eye-contact or many other of even the most elementary, pragmatic, interactional skills. Their language develops slowly, with some problems with using pronouns appropriately, for example. Also, they seem to have a certain fascination with reading, and will often read compulsively, even to reading the dates and other non-essential secondary information on government forms to be filled out.

Of course autistic children do not necessarily have low IQs. Cossu and Marshall (1990) report the case of a retarded Italian third grader (age nine) with a full scale IQ of forty-seven. Despite extremely poor abilities in many neuropsychological areas (such as copying figures, and memory for numbers), his spoken language was normal for expression, although his auditory comprehension was quite poor. Nevertheless, he had learned to read with no extra tutoring in his class, and indeed, in third grade, was considered the best reader in the class when reading-aloud tasks were required. Cossu and Marshall strongly argue that, if a minimum IQ is necessary to acquire reading skills, then it is less than forty-seven, which is substantially below the range of normal (which starts at eighty and averages one hundred). Of course by reading skills here, they mean the ability to phonologically decode written language, not the ability to glean meaning from it.

Child dyslexics, by definition, have no history of frank, neurological problems. Some students of childhood language disorders have observed that children with recurrent ear infections in early childhood may develop difficulties with spoken language or with learning to read, presumably because they did not get the full input about the phonological value of the speech system at a crucial period. Most scholars and clinicians believe that there is additional brain basis for the various forms of childhood dyslexia as well. One piece of evidence is the markedly higher proportion of left-handers among dyslexics and their family members. As Geschwind and Galaburda (1985) pointed out in the theory we discussed in chapter 2, this suggests unusual brain laterality in dyslexics. Also, dyslexia has been reported markedly more frequently among boys than girls. One explanation for this would be, as Geschwind and Galaburda posited, that gender-related hormonal development *in utero* influences cellular migration to language areas as well as handedness. Galaburda and his colleagues (see Rosen, Sherman, and Galaburda, 1993) have been able to perform a series of postmortem studies on individuals who were dyslexics as children, and have found unusually *over*developed right hemispheres in all of them, as well as unusual cellular clusters in exactly the brain areas understood to be involved in reading. The overdevelopment of the right hemisphere may account for the special talents that are often found in dyslexics for so-called "right-hemisphere" skills mentioned in chapter 7 such as the visual arts.

Alexia

How we know what brain areas are involved in reading is through studies of alexics. From 2000 years ago there is evidence of people who had particular difficulties with reading after some form of brain damage. As a higher percentage of the world has become literate in recent centuries, we have reports of more and more cases of individuals with reading problems after brain damage. Sometimes these reading problems seem to be secondary to other sorts of language problems (for example, agrammatics will, as a rule, have particular trouble reading functors as they do in producing them in speech). Most interesting to neurolinguistics, have been cases of "pure alexia" in which the reading problem is the only (or virtually the only) language problem that is seen. Even writing is spared, although the patient cannot monitor what is written as normals do, by reading it over. The case reported by Hinshelwood (1902), an ophthalmologist who became interested in reading disorders, serves as a good example. The patient was a well-educated Englishman who had learned French, as well as Greek and Latin. After a stroke at age 34, the patient was virtually unable to read English, although his reading of Latin was quite spared; that of Greek was somewhat worse, and French was only somewhat better than English. Otherwise he had no primary language disturbance.

The traditional classification system

As cases of pure alexia were reported over the first century of neurolinguistic study, it appeared that several different types could be characterized. Some patients evidenced "letter by letter" reading, that is they could not recognize words or higher units, but they could recognize individual letters. When they spelled these aloud or to themselves (or learned to copy them into their hand in order to get sensory input), they could remember what the letters spelled and therefore say the words. Clearly the problem for them was an input one – they had problems with written but not auditory input of letter strings, resulting in the curious spared ability to read small parts of words but not whole words. By contrast, another set of alexics were unable to read letters but were relatively able to read whole words. In this sort of alexia (sometimes called literal alexia), grammatical functors and nonsense words (that is, words that could exist in a language but do not – e.g. "brub" in English) are more poorly read than substantives. Some patients who cannot read letters have no difficulty with numbers. Moreover, some literal alexics have little difficulty with reading aloud short nonsense words.

These classical subtypings of reading problems reflect the hierarchical organization of orthographies. The lowest level of analysis is the letter; the next level is the word, and the highest level is the sentence. Clearly these levels only apply to written systems that use some form of phoneme (sound) system to convert to graphemes (letters). However, pure alexia has been reported in readers of syllabic and ideographic writing systems as well. In the case of writing systems like that for Chinese, where each symbol represents more or less the equivalent of a word, dyslexics may no longer be able to produce the oral word form, or comprehend its meaning. In a complex orthography like that for Japanese, which includes "kanji" (whole word symbols for most substantives) and "kana" (syllabic forms for functors and borrowed foreign words) alexics have been reported who have difficulty with one but not the other subsystem.

From early this century, it became clear that for pure alexia two brain lesions were required, one to the left occipital lobe so that written information into the left hemisphere could not be passed on to left-hemisphere language areas, and one to the back portion of the corpus callosum, so that the written information that did get in to the right hemisphere also could not be passed to left-hemisphere language areas (see Figure 9.1).

The modern cognitive neuropsychological classification system

With the development of cognitive neuropsychology in recent decades, theorists have developed a new classification system for reading disturbances that follow brain damage.

The two primary types of theoretical interest are surface dys-

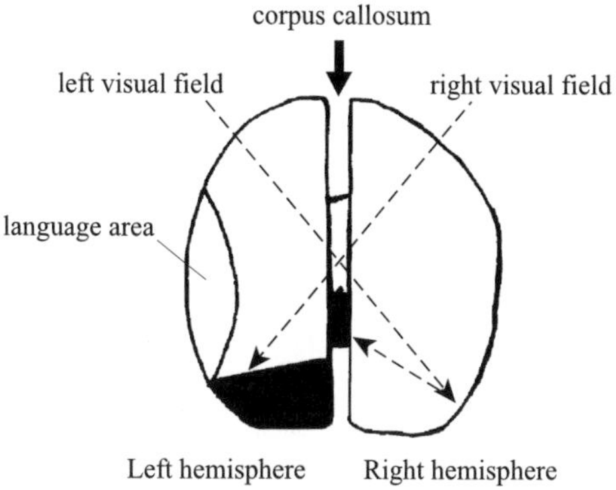

Figure 9.1 The lesions resulting in alexia without agraphia. The lesions are in black. Information from the right visual field cannot get to the language area because of damage to the left occipital lobe. Nor can information from the left visual field get to the language area; it gets to the right occipital lobe but cannot cross to the left hemisphere because of damage to the corpus callosum.

lexia and deep dyslexia. *Surface dyslexics* are able to decode words phonologically, but are not able to recognize whole words. In languages like English, where only some words can be read through "regular" spelling rules, such patients are observed to read regular words correctly and even read nonsense words correctly, but to be unable to read irregular words correctly. What these patients do is regularize the pronunciation of the letter strings, reading "strayigt" for *straight*, for example.

By contrast, *deep dyslexics* are unable to decode words phonologically. The young child learning to read encountering a new word, e.g. "said," will decode it: /sæ-Id/; deep dyslexics are unable to perform this task. This means they are unable to correctly read any non-words, or real words that they have never encountered. They do, however, perform some sort of whole-word or "gestalt" reading of words and as a result they make interesting semantic errors. For example, they may see the word *orchestra* and read it aloud as "symphony." The psychological reality of the orthographic lexicon itself is evident from the fact that even those dyslexics who cannot read non-words can sort words from non-words that look quite similar to words (e.g. *leud* and *lend*).

Several other characteristics are associated with deep dyslexia, although no one has proposed a unified explanation for them. Patients with deep dyslexia will often have greater difficulty in reading functors than substantives, and will sometimes make errors on derivational (as well as inflectional) affixes – the ones that turn words into related words of another word class (e.g. "nation," "national") – either omitting (or adding) them inappropriately or substituting one for another.

Some theorists have worried about why "visual errors" are found among the deep dyslexics as such errors would not seem to be logically linked to the other symptoms. Kaufman and Obler (1993a and b) noted that when normal expert readers make reading errors on single words, these are virtually always words that are visually related to their targets (e.g. "tourists" for "terrorists") and thus it is not surprising that alexics of all sorts, including deep dyslexics, may make them with some frequency when attempting to read whole words.

Cognitive psychologists have been interested in developing a model of how the psycholinguistic process of reading operates based on the sorts of reading patterns they see in such patients. The existence of deep and surface dyslexic patients has been used to argue for a "dual route" model for normal reading, whereby most normal proficient readers can decode words phonologically if necessary, but will also recognize whole words and derive meaning from them without phonological decoding. The sort of flow-chart diagram that John Morton (1979) proposed when he developed the notion of a system of word-form images that was accessed in reading has been modified by these theorists to describe the sequential processes they believe are necessary for reading a word aloud (see Figure 9.2). (Of course they grant that for most normals, reading involves much more than reading single words, but they believe that the processes involved in single word reading are basic.)

In the 1980s this linear model came under substantial attack by "connectionist theorists" who argued that brain processes, including reading, do not operate in linear, modular fashion, but rather with numerous processes working in parallel. They used computers to simulate the way that children learn to read and the way that adults actually read. The evidence they cited was the

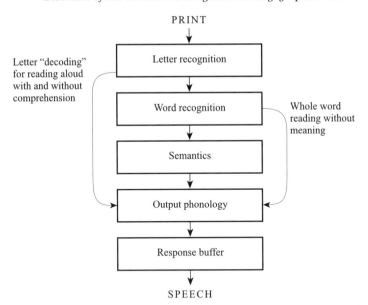

Figure 9.2 A linear model of reading aloud.

"gang" or "neighborhood" effects that render reading of words like *mint* which have a lot of "neighbors" with similar pronunciation (*lint*, *hint*, etc.) faster and earlier learned than "isolated" words like *pint* which lack such "community support." Linguists have, of course, recognized that this type of "analogizing" operates as languages change over the centuries (consider the difference between Chaucer's English and our own) but analogy has not commonly been considered a linguistic component of language processing in individual humans.

For linguists the data on dissociations in brain-damaged patients with reading disorders are of interest in that they suggest factors involved in organizing the lexicon. The distinction among some patients between reading functors and substantives, for example, is further evidence that these words are organized in different subcomponents. One patient, an agrammatic, reported his difficulties with reading functors as "little words—no."

A distinction between abstract and concrete words has also been reported, whereby concrete words (e.g. *library*) are easier to read than words that are matched in all other respects but are abstract (e.g. *liberty*), suggesting that these may be organized differently in the lexicon.

Finally there has been a series of articles on affix-stem relationships in the lexicon. Data from dyslexics complement those from psycholinguistic studies of normals to suggest that stems have status independent from their prefixes and suffixes in the lexicon. This is seen, for example, when patients misread words by reading the stem correctly but substitute one inflectional affix for another, reading "tempted" for "tempts" for example, or vice versa.

Reading problems in different orthographic systems

The question arises as to whether such sorts of reading disabilities can be seen in languages of varying orthographic systems. For example, Spanish, unlike English, has a highly regular phoneme-to-grapheme conversion system. In principle, any one who has mastered this system can read the language aloud, even without understanding what they read. Childhood dyslexia for readers in such languages seems to result mostly in very slow reading, presumably because those children who would achieve whole word reading status must rely on phonological decoding for longer periods (e.g. Wimmer, 1993).

One might expect not to find deep dyslexics among Spanish-speaking, brain-damaged individuals since Spanish orthography can always be easily decoded; there are no irregularly spelled words. Yet Ruiz, Ansaldo, and Lecours, 1994, have reported two cases of deep dyslexia in Spanish (one patient, for example, would read the word *balcón* [meaning balcony] as "terraza" [terrace], or the verb *existir* [to exist] as "ser" [the verb *to be*]). The existence of such individuals suggests that even while a Spanish reader *might* rely on phonological decoding for reading, in fact educated readers with practice will use whole-word-recognition skills as well.

As to surface dyslexia, Coltheart and his colleagues have pointed out that researchers may find evidence of it among readers of languages with virtually transparent sound–letter correspondences. In Spanish, for example, *haza* (an agricultural field) and *asa* (handle) are homophonous, Masterson, Coltheart, and Meara (1985) point out. The bilingual Spanish-English speaker they studied evidenced the classic symptom of developmental surface dyslexia in English: worst reading of irregularly spelled words. In Spanish he could not have this problem, but he had a similar one that also was seen in English; in reading for comprehension he would mistake one member of a homophone pair for another e.g. *haza* for *asa*.

For a language like Chinese, whose written system is called logographic, where individual characters refer quite frequently to whole words, one might expect deep dyslexia to be relatively common (because one might get the semantic nature of a character but speak a different semantically related word), but surface dyslexia not to occur. It turns out, however, that many Chinese characters have a component, called a radical, that indicates their pronounciation. If we consider words containing such logographs as regular, and the ones where such a radical does not indicate the pronounciation as irregular, Yin and Butterworth (1992) point out, it is not difficult to find alexic Chinese readers who make regularization errors but make virtually no semantic errors.

Breakdown in writing

Writing is even more difficult to do than reading – at least for a system like that of English – because, in principle, two alternative routes are available for reading (the phonological decoding route, and the whole word recognition route), but for writing one needs to get the spelling correct. Perhaps 50% of the words of English are irregularly spelled; the requirement to know each word's exact spelling is arduous. Thus, with respect to children there has been some debate as to whether reading and writing disorders may be dissociated from each other, and in particular, whether spelling disorders may occur independent of reading disorders.

With respect to the question of whether one can have a dissociated spelling disorder, the answer seems to be that even college students who have compensated for reading problems can be induced to betray them under testing conditions. Joshi and Aaron (1991), for example, tested three college students who turned up at a spelling clinic asserting their only problem was with spelling. However, it appears that all three had difficulty reading non-words and made substitution errors for functors when reading aloud.

In some severely impaired adult patients, only "automatic" writing is spared, usually the ability to sign their name. For less impaired patients, the types of writing breakdown we discussed earlier in this chapter are seen. Surface dysgraphic problems arise when patients can no longer sound out how non-words should be spelled. Deep dysgraphic problems arise for patients who are asked to write one word and write a semantically related one instead. Caramazza and Hillis (1991) give the example of a patient, K.E., a well-educated fifty-two-year-old with left-hemisphere brain damage, who made semantic errors across many modalities in writing. When asked to write *stapler* to dictation, he wrote "scissors." When shown a picture of the stapler and asked to write its name, he wrote "paper." And when permitted to feel a stapler without seeing it, he wrote "paper clip."

In patients with Alzheimer's disease, writing can be seen to break down in numerous ways. Spelling errors include additions and omissions of letters, substitutions of letters, and spelling regularizations. In addition, words can be illegible or irrelevant and words, phrases or sentences can be inappropriately repeated. Henderson and colleagues (1992) found that all writing errors were particularly linked to problems with visual perceptual tasks as well as the general stage of decline of Alzheimer's disease. Interestingly, as others have found, a substantial number of the spelling errors are made on irregularly spelled words and the corrections are to regularized forms (e.g. *floor* spelled as "flore"). We must conclude that the phoneme-to-grapheme correspondences remain in Alzheimer's disease longer than does memory for the individual irregularly spelled words of which there are so many in English.

Conclusion

Because reading and writing require virtually all the skills of oral language in addition to those of decoding and encoding orthographic information, it is no surprise that there are a number of patterns in which they can break down. Nor is it unexpected that additional brain pathways will be implicated in the breakdown. Geschwind's discovery of the two-part lesion involved in pure alexia is particularly elegant. Many brain lesions, both within the language area and in areas subserving it, will result in difficulties with writing, as the system is vulnerable to many sorts of breakdown at many points.

10 Bilingualism

The ability to speak two or more languages, of course, does not constitute brain damage, and that is why we have reserved this chapter for the last chapter of populations studied. From the neurolinguist's perspective, however, the monolingual may be considered the "unmarked" case of brain organization for language, and the bilingual an interesting modification that pushes us further to think about what we know about the ways the brain can be organized for language. Bilinguals, of course, are not immune to brain damage, and we have referred to some of the bilingual phenomena that may arise in the various forms of brain damage discussed in earlier chapters. In this chapter, we will first discuss definitions of bilingualism, and then review some of the phenomena of normal bilingual language processing that reveal interesting aspects of how the brain can be organized for language, before turning to a section on bilingual aphasics.

Defining bilingualism

Definitions of bilingualism cover a very broad spectrum of linguistic abilities. Perhaps the most liberal definition of the bilingual is "a speaker of one language who can speak in another language." Clearly this definition fits the person who speaks two languages equally fluently. It would, however, also fit the person who has finished less than a single term of study of a second or foreign language. Language learners may be able to construct complete and meaningful utterances in the new language but they may do so in much the same way as they follow recipes or assemble a new bicycle according to written instructions. That is to say, a person who has not yet acquired a full grammar for a language may still be able to construct meaningful utterances in that language. Conversely, the person who is able to read another language fluently with native-like comprehension, may not have learned to *produce* meaningful utterances in that language. This person would not be considered a bilingual by the liberal definition above. A more stringent definition of *bilingual*; "a person with native-like control of two languages," would of course exclude the beginning language student. Such a definition would still exclude the person who easily comprehends but does not produce utterances in a second language. It would also exclude the fluent speaker who had a "foreign accent."

Both extremes in definition yield unsatisfactory results, perhaps because each relies on degree of control of the language as the definitional criterion. A more intuitively appealing definition of *bilingualism* considers the most relevant factor to be the regular *use* of two languages (e.g. François Grosjean, 1982). Regular use of two languages implies a system – or two – of rules for interpreting and possibly producing utterances in both languages. (A mechanism for deciding which language is being heard must also be a necessary component of the comprehension system.) The system for each language may be quite close to the grammar of a monolingual speaker of that language or it may be somewhat different, but surely it is governed by its own set of internally consistent rules. In this chapter we are interested in a broad range of bilingualism-related phenomena, including aspects of acquiring the second language as well as end-state knowledge that is acquired in "balanced" bilinguals, that is, individuals who sound like native speakers of both languages.

"Foreign accent" and bilingual phonology

The one aspect of bilingualism most commonly noted is the relative ease with which a child acquires two languages simultaneously (or a second language in early childhood). By comparison, adults often struggle to learn the language of a new speech community. The most usual case is for children who learn two languages early in life to sound like native speakers in each of their languages. For adults, the more usual case is for the learners of a second language to always be distinguishable from native speakers. These differences may be found in any or all aspects of the linguistic system. Here we focus on the phonological system.

For virtually all adult second language learners, some differences between the native speaker and the second language learner are the norm. The "foreign accent" is one such difference. Non-native sounding speech can be the result of differences between native- and second-language production at the phonetic, phonemic or suprasegmental levels. Speakers whose two languages share a particular sound may give that sound the same phonetic realization in both of their languages. For example, Italian and English both have a phoneme /t/ which contrasts with the similarly articulated but voiced phoneme /d/. However, the English [t] is generally articulated with the tongue tip at the alveolar ridge whereas the Italian [t] has a more dental articulation.[4] The tendency is for adult learners of either language to maintain the articulation of the sound from their native language.

Another source of "foreign accent" is a difference in the phoneme inventory of the two languages. A sound which is not in the first language may be substituted for by a phonetically similar sound from the first language or an already mastered second language sound. For example, the English sounds [θ] and [ð] are relatively rare in the world's languages. Speakers of English as a second language will often substitute other voiceless/voiced sounds which are close in place and/or manner of articulation (e.g. [s] and [z] or [t] and [d]).

Even if the speaker's two languages have the same sounds, they may differ as to whether two sounds are separate phonemes or allophones of one phoneme. For example, English has two phones [p] and [p^h]. They are in *complementary distribution*, with [p^h] occurring in syllable-initial position and [p] occurring elsewhere. The two phones are allophones of one phoneme /p/. Thai has the same two phones [p] and [p^h], but they are not in complementary distribution. They are allophones of separate phonemes, /p/ and /p^h/. Thus those two sounds can be the only distinguishing factor between two Thai words, for example, /pin/ and /p^{h}in/. The

English speaker learning Thai may tend to use Thai /p/ and/pʰ/ as [p] and [pʰ] are used in English.

If both languages have the same sounds with the same phonemic status, the second-language learner may still experience the "foreign accent phenomenon" if the phonotactic constraints of the two languages differ. For example, both Spanish and English have the phonemes /s/, /t/ and /r/. English permits syllable-initial consonant clusters such as /st/ or /str/. Spanish does not permit such clusters. A Spanish speaker may have no trouble pronouncing an English word such as *estrogen* which conforms to the phonotactic rules of Spanish and English, but have difficulty pronouncing *stress* which violates the phonotactic constraints of Spanish. The German-speaking learner of Swedish encounters pronunciation difficulties in spite of the close relationship between the two languages and the many cognates – i.e. words in the two languages that are related to each other for historical reasons. In German, voiced consonants become devoiced at the ends of words. For example, the word *Bad* "bath" is pronounced /bat/, but the cognate Swedish word *bad* "bath" is pronounced /bad/.

Within the first year of life, children lose the ability to distinguish many of the sounds that need not be distinguished in the specific language they are exposed to. This has been demonstrated for infants by behavioral techniques, and has been verified in adults in studies such as that of Buchwald et al. (1994) who use event-related evoked potentials (ERPs) (see chapter 3, the section on imaging techniques) to demonstrate that Japanese speakers do not show the electrophysiological responses correlating to the distinctions between /r/ and /l/ that the English speakers do.

A foreign accent may also manifest itself in suprasegmental or prosodic elements of pronunciation. For example, English is a stress-timed language with a tendency toward evenly spaced duration between stresses. French is a syllable-timed language with a stress on every syllable. Learning one type of language after becoming proficient in a language of the other type can result in non-native-like intonation patterns in the second language. (Problems with prosody and articulation have been reported in a rare phenomenon associated with aphasia in monolinguals called "foreign accent syndrome." The classic case was reported by

Monrad-Krohn in 1947. The patient was a Norwegian-speaking aphasic who had had no exposure to German but after her aphasia was taken by her compatriots to have a German accent, much to her distress given the politics of the time.)

In short, an examination of second-language phonology reinforces the notions of structure and rule-governedness in human languages. The fact that young children can acquire a second or subsequent language without an accent in any of them is evidence that the human brain – at least before some "critical" or "sensitive" period – is capable of developing two or more different sets of instructions for the organs of articulation. We may ask if the average adult learner who does exhibit a foreign accent is simply using the brain representation for the first language when speaking the second or subsequent language or whether perhaps a second system is developed which is, however, not identical to the system developed by native speakers. A closer examination of issues of phonological perception and production in balanced bilinguals provides some answers to this question.

As we said above, a balanced bilingual is a person who is equally fluent and accent-free in both languages. There exists a small but convincing body of literature that demonstrates that even for balanced bilinguals, some aspects of the phonological systems of their languages are more unitary than separate. For example, Obler (1982) looked at the production of stops in ten balanced Hebrew-English bilinguals. They were tested on their production of [p]/[b], [t]/[d] and [k]/[g] before vowels in Hebrew on one day and in English on another. Although these stop pairs are articulated similarly in the two languages, there is a difference as to when the vocal cords begin to vibrate relative to the release of the stop closure (voice onset time or VOT). The table below (Table 10.1) shows the average VOT for the ten balanced bilinguals as well as the monolingual Hebrew and monolingual English controls. Taking the [p]/[b] pair as an example, we see that the Hebrew speakers have an earlier VOT for both the [p] and [b] relative to the monolingual English speakers. This means that the Hebrew [p] has less "aspiration" than the English [p] and that the Hebrew [b] is more fully voiced than the English [b]. The bilinguals as a group *did* use a different VOT for their [p] and [b] sounds when speaking Hebrew vs. English.

Table 10.1. *Voice onset time means for stop-consonant production by Hebrew-English bilinguals*

Measurement of milliseconds before (negative numbers) or after (positive numbers) the stop burst

	Unilinguals		Bilinguals	
	Hebrew group	English group	Hebrew condition	English condition
/p/	+ 25.6	+ 77.6	+ 58.0	+ 68.8
/b/	− 110.8	− 8.5	− 96.8	− 64.8
/t/	+ 33.9	+ 77.0	+ 73.8	+ 89.6
/d/	− 95.8	− 6.8	− 85.5	− 55.8
/k/	+ 63.7	+ 89.4	+93.2	+99.4
/g/	− 101.0	+15.1	−92.2	−58.3

Note: Reprinted from L. K. Obler, The Parsimonious Bilingual, in L. K. Obler and L. Menn, eds., *Exceptional Language and Linguistics*, New York, NY: Academic Press, 1982.

However, in both languages, their mean VOT was significantly different from that of the monolingual controls. As Table 10.1 indicates, the bilinguals seemed to be opting for VOTs which maximized the differences between the voiced and voiceless phonemes across the two languages. They produced very voiced [b] sounds in both languages, with somewhat earlier voicing when speaking Hebrew. They produced very aspirated [p] sounds in both languages with slightly earlier voicing when speaking Hebrew.

These same bilinguals were tested on their perception of voiced and voiceless stops using synthetic sounds ranging in VOT from 150 msc. before the stop closure to 150 msc. after the stop closure. Since Hebrew voiced and voiceless stops have an earlier VOT than the corresponding English stops, monolingual speakers of Hebrew stopped consistently labelling the artificially produced stops "b" at an earlier VOT and began consistently labelling stops "p" at an earlier VOT. The bilingual subjects did have different voiced/voiceless cut-off points when tested in English than when tested in

Hebrew. However, the differences between the two languages of the bilinguals were not as great as the differences between the two groups of monolinguals. Also, the breaking points between the voiced and voiceless stops were farther apart for the bilinguals than the monolinguals. This meant that the bilinguals had a greater period of uncertainty; a range of VOTs in which a stop might be considered either voiced or voiceless. The bilinguals seemed to have a broad, unitary system for perception of sounds; somewhere between the two monolingual norms.

The bilingual lexicon

The question of "two systems or one" resurfaces at each level of analysis of bilingual language behavior. If the vocabulary of a native speaker is understood to be organized in a mental lexicon according to phonological as well as semantic principles, how then is the bilingual's vocabulary represented? There are a number of logical possibilities, some of which are illustrated in Figure 10.1.

The two lexicons, and, more generally, the two linguistic systems of the bilingual are undoubtedly neither entirely separate nor entirely joined. For two decades (in the 1960s and the 1970s) a large number of psycholinguistic studies of the lexicon of bilinguals would demonstrate either that there was one "compound," that is, unified system or two "coordinate," that is, parallel, systems, depending on the tasks that were used for testing (see review in Albert and Obler, 1978). One thing is certain, however, that bilinguals are able to maintain separation between their two languages for many purposes. For example, when addressing a monolingual speaker of one of their languages, bilinguals are normally able to speak exclusively in that language. This has led some researchers (e.g. Macnamara, 1967) to propose that the grammars of a bilingual were controlled by a "switch" which could be consciously set for one language or the other. Instances when a bilingual is surprised to be accidentally addressing a monolingual in the "wrong" language are quite rare. The intrusion of a word from the "wrong" language when a bilingual is experiencing some word-finding difficulty is more common, however, and causes some difficulty for the "switch" theory.

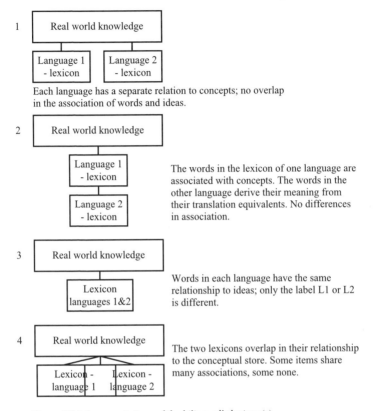

Figure 10.1 Representations of the bilingual's lexicon(s).

Experimental findings also pose difficulties for the "switch" model. There is a type of psycholinguistic test called the Stroop test. In this test, subjects name the color of the ink of a series of rectangles on plain cards. This provides baseline data on the amount of time required for the subject to complete the naming task. Afterwards the subject is asked to perform the same task, naming the ink color on a series of cards. However, this time, the ink spells the name of a color other than the ink color. For example, one card might have the word *green* spelled out in red ink. The correct response to that card is "RED." In general, subjects are able to perform this task with a high degree of accuracy, seldom saying the written word rather than the ink color. Their response times are, however, much slower. This means that although consciously the subjects know that the color word is irrelevant to the task at hand, unconsciously they are processing the meaning of that word.

In the bilingual version of this task, the color naming is in one of the bilingual's languages and the distractor words are in the other. In spite of the fact that the color words are not in the same language that the bilingual is using to name the ink colors, naming speed is affected. It is interesting to note that if a "wrong" answer is given it is usually a translation of the printed color word into the language of the color-naming task. For example if a French/English bilingual were taking the test, the response to the word *jaune* written in blue ink would most likely be a somewhat delayed but correct "blue." The next most likely response is "yellow," an English translation of the French distractor.

The mutual effects of the lexicons of the bilingual can also be seen in other contexts. Haravon, Obler and Gerstman (1991) conducted a study on the evaluation of the positive and negative connotations of words by Spanish/English balanced bilinguals. They chose words which have strong positive or negative connotations in one language and a *false* cognate with neutral or opposite valence in the other. For example, English *embarrassed* looks and sounds like Spanish *embarazada* ("pregnant") but has, obviously, quite a different meaning. Neutral words which had strongly negative, false cognates were rated significantly more negatively by the bilinguals than they were by the monolingual controls. It is important to note that this does not indicate any confusion on the part of the bilingual subjects as to the actual meanings of the "sound-alike" words in their two languages. It does demonstrate that the two systems may influence each other.

Over an extended period of language contact in a bilingual community, a word may take on a new meaning based on the meaning of a word in the other language which originally shared other senses. This process is known as "calqueing." For example, English *run* and Spanish *correr* share the meaning "to go by moving the legs rapidly" in all varieties of Spanish and English. In

English, *run* can also be used in another sense: to attempt to be elected to an office, as in "She is running for Governor." In most varieties of Spanish, *correr* cannot be used in this sense. However, in the Spanish/English bilingual community in New York City, *correr* has taken on this political sense.

Garro (1992) devised a psycholinguistic test to investigate the effect of calqued senses on the organization of the Spanish mental dictionary of Spanish/English bilinguals in New York City. Her subjects all spoke Spanish natively. Her controls were monolingual speakers of a non-contact variety of Spanish. The task used by Garro was a semantic priming task. Recall that in English, hearing the word "exercise" should make reaction times to the word *run* faster. The word "election" should also prime the word *run*. Garro found that for her bilingual subjects but not the monolingual controls, the Spanish words which had developed new senses based on English models were primed by Spanish words related to that new sense (e.g. *elección/correr* "election/run"). In other words, exposure to a new lexicon had caused changes in the mental representation and patterns of interconnection in the lexicon of the first language. Davidson and Schwartz (1994) report a similar phenomenon among bidialectal speakers of Jamaican English and New York English. In standard American English, the word *tomato* refers to a red fruit, commonly thought of as a vegetable, that can be used in salads along with other foods. In Jamaican patois, the word *salad* simply refers to the red vegetable. Native speakers of Jamaican patois who immigrate to areas where Standard English is spoken are more likely to think of tomatoes when given the English word *salad* than are unidialectal speakers of Standard English, even though tomatoes are frequently part of the prototypic salad for them.

Code-switching

In addition to speaking two or more languages fluently, many bilinguals have another rather interesting ability; that is, the ability to employ elements of both languages when speaking with another bilingual. This is known as *code-switching*. The following examples cited in Garro (1992) illustrate typical kinds of switches.

The stretches of speech in each language are syntactically and phonologically appropriate for that language:

> You didn't have to worry *que* somebody *te iba a tirar con cerveza o una botella* or something like that.
> "You didn't have to worry that somebody was going to throw beer or a bottle at you or something like that." (Poplack, 1981: 170. Cited in Garro [1992].)

> So you *todavia* haven't decided *lo que vas a hacer* next week.
> "So you still haven't decided what you are going to do next week." (Poplack, Wheeler & Westwood, 1987: 34–35. Cited in Garro [1992].)

Like all linguistic behavior, code-switching is governed by internalized rules. Switches are never made at points in the sentence where switching would leave some portion of the string unacceptable in the language of that portion. For example, in the figure below taken from Poplack (1980) by Nishimura (1986) a switch between *no* and *take* would leave the English verb phrase unmarked for tense and is therefore not a permissible switch. Researchers such as Poplack, working with closely related languages such as Spanish and English, proposed that there was no one base language for bilingual discourse with code-switching. Instead, speakers create sentence structures by combining phrase structure rules from the two languages. Both languages are simultaneously available for perception and production. Switches are permitted whenever the relative order of the constituents is the same across the two languages. Other researchers (see Nishimura (1990) for a review) have felt it important to name a base language for each stretch of discourse. When working with languages with very different phrase structure (e.g. Japanese and English), a model based on properly ordered constituents from one language being grafted into a phrase structure tree generated by the grammar of the other language seems to fit the switching data better. Even this model requires the simultaneous availability of both grammars.

One question that has arisen is whether the bilingual's brain, through practice, has developed abilities that no monolingual's has, or whether, rather, the bilingual's special abilities are built on those that all monolinguals have, such as the ability to switch linguistic "register" as one speaks differently to a young child and

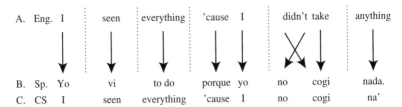

Figure 10.2 Permissible code-switching points within the framework of Sankoff and Poplack, 1980. Switching would be possible at any syntactic sites marked by dotted lines, since the relative order of constituents at these sites is common in Spanish and English. The actual performance of the speaker is represented in C.

a professional colleague in the same conversation. Mahecha et al. (1992) demonstrated that, at least for bilinguals' ability to appreciate subtle phonological cues that predict code-switches, monolinguals, while insensitive to these without instruction to listen to them, could quickly be brought up to the bilinguals' performance with instruction. This suggests that there are no qualitative distinctions between the language processing of bilinguals and monolinguals.

Individual differences in second language acquisition abilities

The ability to learn a second language as an adult varies considerably from person to person. Most people who acquire a second language after puberty may attain a fair degree of grammatical competence and lexical knowledge, but still have at least an accent. Few individuals have been studied who do acquire native-like abilities after puberty, even though this should not be possible according to the critical period hypothesis of Lenneberg discussed in chapter 6. One example is C.J., studied by Novoa, Fein, and Obler (1988).

C.J. was an American high-school student before he was exposed to any foreign languages, but he succeeded well beyond most of his peers. In high school he studied German as well as French; in college he was a French major and spent a year in France, visiting Germany briefly. After college he took a job in

Morocco and, he reported, quickly picked up Moroccan Arabic through both formal and informal instruction. On neuro-psychological tests, C.J. showed a particular ability to remember the forms of things as distinct from their content. Not surprisingly, he was particularly good at verbal memory (although merely normal at other sorts of memory like remembering spatial patterns).

As to the theories that having a "musical ear" or good analytic syntactic abilities account for good second language learning, C.J. performed merely normally on musical tasks and on parsing grammatical structures, a metalinguistic syntactic task. More bilateral brain organization for language may have helped him: C.J. was a left-hander and showed no particular cognitive style that might be termed "left hemisphere" or "right hemisphere" on Edith Kaplan's task in which subjects are asked first to visualize and name all the letters of the alphabet that rhyme with "tree", the more "left-hemisphere style" task, and then to visualize the alphabet and name the capital letters with curves in them, the "right-hemisphere style" task. Despite average to high-average performance on the standard Wechsler IQ test (with better performance on verbal than non-verbal components), C.J. performed particularly well on a task called Raven's progressive matrixes, which is a strictly non-verbal task requiring appreciation of patterns.

Novoa et al. (1988) argue that C.J.'s case provides an example of a particular talent, in this instance talented second-language acquisition, being linked to the Geschwind-Galaburda hypothesis that links neurological, immunological, and endocrinological factors during gestation to talents and lack of abilities throughout development, in that he not only was a left-hander but also is a twin, is homosexual, and was somewhat delayed in reading.

Schneiderman and Desmarais (1988) formulated specific hypotheses based on the Geschwind-Galaburda hypothesis and this study to test the extent to which such biological underpinnings of language talent would hold. They hypothesized that several aspects of neurocognitive ability would be greater in exceptionally talented second-language learners than in normal controls. In a study of two subjects they demonstrated that their talented learners did not show the usual pattern of left dominance for language lateralization, performed substantially better on verbal than on non-verbal tasks, were particularly good at acquiring new codes, and, as Novoa et al. (1988) had predicted, did not use standard categories as a strategic aid in memory tasks.

Second-language learning ability and IQ

One thing is certain; second-language learning ability is independent of general intellectual ability. This is demonstrated particularly clearly in a series of publications (e.g., Smith and Tsimpli, 1991), about the translation abilities of a "savant-linguist" referred to as "Christopher" in the articles. Christopher is institutionalized because his general intellectual abilities do not allow him to take care of himself. He has a non-verbal IQ of sixty to seventy. Yet he has a remarkable ability to learn new languages. In addition to English, which is his native language, Christopher has acquired a fairly high degree of proficiency in French, German, Spanish and Modern Greek. He also knows *twelve* other languages well enough to provide translations into English. As is demonstrated in the excerpts below, some of his translations are much more true to the text than others. Still, it is fair to say that there are very few people even with normal or superior intellectual ability who could do as much with passages from sixteen languages:

Danish   Men Jeg havde hverken onkler eller tenter i København, så jeg kom først dertil, da jeg var så stor, at jeg gik i skole og vidste, at det var Danmarks hovedstad og den største og vigtigste by i landet.

Fair translation: But I had neither uncles nor aunts in Copenhagen, so I didn't get to go there until I was old enough to be at school and learnt that Copenhagen was the capital of Denmark and the biggest and most important city in the country.

C's translation: but I had neither uncles nor niece – nor aunts – in Copenhagen, so I came first there as I was a very big man, when I went to school and knew that it was Denmark's capital and the biggest and importantest – and the most important town in the whole country.

French   Nous faisions pique-nique au bord de la route nationale qui s'étendait devant nous, toute droite et bordée d'arbres.

Fair translation: We were having a picnic beside the main road which stretched away in front of us; dead straight and lined with trees.

C's translation: We had a picnic at the route, at the board of the road, which which ran behind us, straight and full of trees.

It is also clear from these passages that Christopher's abilities extend beyond the memorization of translation equivalents. In each of his more developed languages he is able to give consistent well-formedness judgments and to make corrections to ill-formed strings. Based on their study of Christopher's emerging grammar of Modern Greek, Smith and Tsimpli conclude that Christopher's grammar, although different from that of native speakers of Greek in important ways, is rule-governed.

Bilingual aphasics

The information about speech and language in healthy bilinguals speaks to the issue of joined versus separate linguistic systems but does not directly address the issue of shared brain space. Bilingual aphasics have been a source of information regarding the localization of the bilingual's two grammars. If the linguistic abilities in each language were subserved by the same brain tissue, we would expect that whenever there was damage to the language area of the brain, equivalent deficits would be found in each language. As we noted in chapter 4, this is not always the case. However, when Charlton (1964) studied nine unselected bilingual aphasic cases who came into his service, he found that such parallel deficits and recoveries were the rule for seven of them. In a systematic review of the existing literature on aphasia in bilinguals, Paradis (1987) found that more than half of the cases reported involved patients whose languages were equally deficited by their brain injury and whose languages recovered to the same extent.

Naturally for the cases that do show recovery, there is a selection bias for publication. Those cases which are written up are the more interesting cases. These are likely to be the cases of non-parallel recovery which are of interest in that they demonstrate that, at least in some humans, differential processing of the two languages of the bilingual is wired into the brain.

In bilingual patients whose languages do not recover in parallel fashion, there are a number of distinct recovery patterns. Some patients recover one language after the other. Some patients never recover one of their languages. One famous case is the Swiss-born patient of Minkowski (described in Minkowski, 1927). Swiss-German was his first language. He spoke some Italian and had learned Standard German in school. French was his most frequently used language at the time of his stroke. All of his other languages recovered to some extent except Swiss-German. In spite of spending his last years in a Swiss-German-speaking environment, his native tongue never recovered. A tumor patient tested by one of us (LKO) actually had a fluent aphasia in her fourth language (Hebrew), and a non-fluent aphasia in her third language (English). In her first (Hungarian) and second (French) languages she was moderately fluent (Albert and Obler, 1978).

Two major theories dominated the literature of the past century on which language would return first in bilingual aphasics, the first-learned language (the theory of Ribot) or the language that had been most used around the time of the aphasia-producing incident (the theory of Pitres, 1895). Individual authors would collect several cases that supported one or the other theory and write that, based on these cases, that was the theory that held. Some authors posited yet a third pattern, when neither of the other two was the one that held, namely that "psychological" factors dominated which language would return first. For example, Minkowski (1928) reported the case of a Swiss-German man who spoke French as the first language after his injury to everyone's surprise; French had been the language of his first important love affair.

Because these three theories are not mutually exclusive, LKO analyzed all the cases we could locate (over a hundred) in the literature on differential impairment and/or recovery from aphasia statistically (Obler and Albert, 1977), and found that initial recovery of the first-learned language occurs at no greater than chance levels, while initial recovery of the most recently used languages does occur significantly more often than chance would predict. Naturally we could not test the third "psychological" theory, as one can always develop a psychological explanation for whatever language returns first. We may conclude, then, that recent brain activation, in terms of what has been happening, linguistically speaking, in the years prior to an aphasia-producing incident, is an important factor in determining how language is produced after the aphasia.

One pattern of recovery that Paradis et al. (1987) have demonstrated he calls "alternate antagonism." In such a case the patient, early after the aphasia-producing accident, is able to speak only one language for a period, say a day, and then, the following day, can speak only the other language. Green (1986) has developed a theory to account for such cases and other cases of differential recovery which argues that the underlying problem for these bilingual aphasics is not that one or the other language has been "lost," but rather that with limited resources the patient is no longer able to switch back and forth between the two or more languages.

Lateral dominance

There have been dozens of laterality studies conducted on normal bilinguals in the past thirty years debating whether there is more right-hemisphere involvement among bilinguals in general than among monolinguals, or for the second or less proficient language as compared to the first. As we mentioned in chapter 3, tachistoscopic and dichotic tests in normal monolinguals are somewhat problematic; in bilinguals the problems are compounded by difficulties in, for example, setting up comparable stimuli in both languages, and selecting subjects with equivalent language-learning histories (Obler et al., 1982).

Vaid (1983) provided a useful evaluation of this bilingual laterality literature and concluded that age of acquisition is most crucial in determining lateral organization for bilingualism: late bilinguals are more likely to show increased right hemisphere involvement in language processing. Further evidence in support of this point comes from Wuillemin and Richardson (1994). They used a form of tachistoscopic presentation whereby Papua New Guinean University students were tested reading words presented to their left or right visual fields, both for English as a second language and for Tok Pisin as a second language. For both these structurally quite different languages, response times to words presented in the left visual field were greater than those for the right visual field (suggesting left-hemisphere dominance) for individuals who learned their second language before the age of four. For individuals who had learned it between nine and twelve, however, somewhat reversed performance was seen, suggesting rather more right-hemisphere participation.

Cortical stimulation

With cortical stimulation techniques, you will recall (chapter 3), we can learn about areas within the language area where lexical access is blocked by brief small electrical pulses. In bilingual patients about to undergo surgery, this technique can tell us about within-hemisphere organization for the two languages. Ojemann and Whitaker (1978), for example, had the opportunity to test one Spanish-English and one Dutch-English adult using the cortical stimulation technique. They found that a language area similar to that for monolinguals existed around the Sylvian fissure of the hemisphere dominant for language. Within that language area, certain points of stimulation disrupted naming in both languages, while others were more likely to disrupt naming in one or the other language. They also speculated that perhaps the areas that seemed to be involved in both languages were those more central ones around the Sylvian fissure while those devoted to one or the other language were more peripheral within the language area. This speculation was supported by Fedio et al. in a similar study of a Spanish-English patient (1992).

Additional evidence for the different but somewhat overlapping organization of a bilingual's languages in the brain comes from the study of Haglund, et al. (1993) on a bilingual speaker of English and American Sign Language (ASL). The subject was tested via cortical stimulation because of her intractable epileptic seizures. Although she was hearing, she had learned ASL while she was a young child because her sister was congenitally deaf. For stimulation within the traditional language area, few points interfered significantly with all language abilities in both languages (naming in English, naming in ASL, and interpreting ASL into English). Only stimulation in the regions around Broca's area seemed to interfere with both English and ASL production. Additionally, stimulation in relatively widespread anterior areas of the temporal lobe resulted in problems with hand shapes in the ASL naming task, and then finger spelling was selectively impaired after surgery in that area. Based on their own study and that of Mateer et al. (1982), the authors conclude that the anterior temporal lobe is more crucial for visual-gestural signing than for spoken languages.

Conclusion

A number of the phenomena of bilingualism seen in normals suggest the intricate ways in which independent systems can be set up for processing phonology, morphosyntax, and lexicon. Yet a certain measure of parsimony seems to enter, in that these systems are only as independent as necessary, and reliance on a single system is the rule whenever possible. From the literature on aphasia and dementia in polyglots, we learn that it is unusual but not impossible for independent systems to be manifested after brain damage. These separate systems appear not to reflect gross distinctions in areas contributing to the performance of the two or more languages, but rather distinctions that may reflect resource allocation. The additional right-hemisphere participation in language processing among normal, late bilinguals may constitute part of this resource allocation. The cortical stimulation literature suggests that while the language area of bilinguals is in the core parts of the cortical left hemisphere, as in monolinguals, subtle distinctions within that area may be linked to bilinguals' separable systems.

11 Language organization

Up to this point in the book, we have been discussing what we know about the individual populations from whom we have gleaned knowledge about neurolinguistics. At the end of each chapter we have provided a conclusion about the brain areas that seem to be impaired for the group studied in that chapter and how the brain damage is related to the language phenomena characteristically seen. In this chapter we pull together information provided in those chapters to focus on the linguistic constructs that have a "psychological reality" apart from their abstract value.

Since Noam Chomsky's 1957 book *Syntactic Structures*, a major goal for modern linguistics has been to construct a model for the grammar of an "ideal" native speaker of a language. The primary goal is to create an abstract model that "generates" – that is, accounts for – all of the grammatical sentences in the language without generating any ungrammatical strings. These models are not *intended* to reflect processes that native speakers use to actually create sentences each time they speak, of course. Some linguists may see the generative grammar as an essential part of a production model; that is, they see the grammar as somehow "driving" actual speech production or comprehension. Many others see the generative grammar as potentially divorced from the speech process. For them, the grammar describes the abstract patterns of the language, while another set of rules that one might call a production grammar tells speakers how to actually speak.

We prefer to assume that our abstract grammar does have some connection to the physical manifestations of speech and language processes. As a result, we would expect that autonomous aspects of analysis could be linked to dissociable kinds of impairment in brain-damaged patients. If performance on one set of linguistic items (e.g. functor words) is markedly impaired but that on related items (e.g. nouns and verbs) is quite spared, this dissociation in performance suggests that the two sets of items are at least psychologically distinct. That is, independent psychological mechanisms must exist for processing them. What is meant by "psychological reality" of an abstract grammatical concept, then, is that it is not only an abstract linguistic concept; it can be seen to operate during speech production and/or comprehension.

This notion of "psychological reality" is an important one for determining the relation between abstract theoretical notions that linguists have deduced and how the brain actually functions. It is conceivable that these abstract notions in fact have their reflections in brain representations and processes. It is, we grant, also possible that the abstract notions describe a pattern that exists in language as an abstract entity, but has no meaningful relation to how language is actually processed. Consider how little relation there is between the mathematical equation that describes the spiral-shape pattern of the seeds at the center of a sunflower, and whatever biological rules govern the seeds patterning into that shape.

Arithmetic is a system in some ways similarly abstract to language. While we may expect some brain representation for the math-facts that we have automatic access to (e.g. $5 + 4 = 9$), we may question whether such abstract principles as commutativity (the rule that tells us that if we add A plus B first and then add C to it, we get the same result as if we add B plus C first and then add A to the sum) are represented as a rule in a distinct location, or even a distinct neural pathway in the brain. Certainly very few of us can articulate that rule (or remember its name), although most adults operate on the understanding that it is true without being able to specify it. We may conclude, based on our real-world use of the principle, that commutativity has psychological reality, but we would not expect it to have a brain location associated with it.

How then does the notion of "psychological reality" speak to the relation between competence and performance? While most linguists are interested in studying competence, as we mentioned above, that is, the elegant underlying grammar of language as we adults know it, we may well ask how our flawed performance relates to this competence. Is there a simple one-to-one relation between the rules of the grammar and the rules we use for speaking or understanding (parsing) what we hear? Or is there an entirely different grammar built for producing language and understanding it, one that may take into account such factors as word-frequency or the likelihood that certain syntactic structures will be employed? Indeed it is conceivable that computer-programming types of principles will predominate in giving us performance grammars that work for production and comprehension and that are substantially distinct from the elegant structures of a competence grammar.

In earlier chapters, we have considered how linguistic notions have proved useful in studying patterns of behavior in brain-damaged individuals. Here we ask how neurolinguistic data buttress aspects of linguistic theory. Most theoretical linguistic discussion arises from linguists' thinking about what appears to be going on and testing out their ideas against native-speaker intuitions of which sentences are grammatical and which are not. Neurolinguistic data, like data from other "exceptional" language performance such as pidgin language or literary language or normal speech errors (Obler and Menn, 1982) permit us a complementary measure to evaluate the linguistic constructs.

In this chapter we will use the basic linguistic levels (phonology, morphology, syntax, semantics) to structure the discussion. After discussing the linguistic notions of competence and performance, we address several phonological concepts (the phoneme, the distinctive feature, morphophonological constraints on word structure, syllable, and the suprasegmentals tone and intonation). We then turn to morphological notions such as the word-group classes, morphophonological concepts such as compounding and affixation and the relation between morphology and syntax. Under syntactic notions we treat the notions of hierarchy and complexity, deep and surface syntax, traces, and thematic role. With respect to theories of how the lexicon is organized, we treat what a lexicon is itself, the notion of word, the distinction between lexical form and semantic meaning, semantic hierarchies, and semantic networks. Under pragmatics we treat conversational rules, Grice's maxims for interpreting conversation, the lexicon of emotion, and bilingual language choice. Vis-à-vis written language systems, we cover the interface between phonology and orthography, the differences between different orthographic types, even for the same language (as in the syllable and whole-word representations in Japanese), the two-route model of normal reading and spelling regularity. Of course these are not all the theoretical concepts that could be extracted from the work in this book; rather, they are a representative sample of concepts that linguists have found useful for which we have neurolinguistic evidence.

Competence and performance

This linguistic distinction between our knowledge of language and our actual use of it has been stressed by linguists to emphasize the importance of focusing on the abstract grammar. It was not intended to enable us to understand even normal speech errors, not to mention the production of brain-damaged subjects. However, we may say that the distinction is made much richer by the literature on language breakdown. It is most strikingly evident in patients whose output is agrammatic, yet who are able to perform quite well on grammaticality judgment tasks. We must assume they have the grammatical knowledge even if they do not appear to be able to use it in their speech. Similarly, we must assume that competence, as linguists think of it, is spared for aphasic patients who have either production or comprehension skills impaired, but not both. Likewise, patients whose only problems are in reading, or in understanding auditory language input, but not both, provide evidence that competence is spared because they have one modality that is functioning.

Phonology

Because units of linguistic analysis are not necessarily physically real, we must evaluate their "psychological reality" by seeing if they make a difference in our speech or comprehension of language.

For example, people do not knowingly speak in phonemes. Speech scientists tell us that a given "phoneme" may be pronounced markedly differently depending on the context it is in. The characteristic sounds composing a /b/ before the vowel /i/ are different from those before a /u/. However, linguists have long understood that both are perceived by the speaker as well as the listener as the "same" sound, and, at least for English speakers, this sound is to be distinguished from a similar one whose voicing starts later, the sound that is produced in similar fashion but with a later onset of vocal cord vibration, namely /p/. Indeed, these two "sounds" equally distinguish the words "cap" and "cab" and the words "pour" and "boar." It is this possibility of recognizing distinctive phonemes that contributes to what we mean by "psychological reality." The distinction is meaningful for the speaker and the listener, and it must be represented in their brains for language processing, even if they are not able to explain the phenomenon without advanced linguistic training!

Each particular instance of a sound in a speech stream has its own collection of features. In the chapter on bilingualism, we discussed Voice Onset Time or VOT, one of the properties of "stops" (i.e. sounds made by using the articulators to "stop" the flow of air from the lungs). Recall that voice onset time refers to the time when the vocal cords begin to vibrate relative to the time the articulators close. The English sounds "p" and "b," for example, are distinguished only by VOT. However, there is no one single VOT associated with each of the two sounds. Instead, native speakers recognize a range of VOTs starting from around sixty milliseconds after the release of the stop as "p" and another range ending around five milliseconds before release of the stop as "b." Distinctions that can be readily discerned by machines, by prelingual infants and by speakers of languages that distinguish three phonemes in this range (e.g. Thai), are routinely ignored by native speakers of English. This "categorical perception" of sounds as phonemes is one of the main arguments from unimpaired speakers in favor of the psychological reality of the phoneme. Further evidence from normals for the meaningfulness of phonemes is that cueing a forgotten word by giving the speaker its first phoneme is often quite successful in eliciting the word.

In the literature we have covered in this book, the psychological reality of phonemes is evidenced most vividly in the phonemic paraphasias of aphasics. Regularly, in this sort of substitution error, it is only one phoneme that has been substituted for or omitted (e.g. *spill* for *spell*). Recall that the equivalent can also be seen in the visual-gestural system, as elements equivalent to phonemes are seen to be substituted for in certain aphasics who are speakers of signed languages.

The fact that some bilinguals often evidence a "foreign accent" in one of their languages, also indicates that specific phonemes have a strong, psychologically real, phonetic identity. The phonetic constraints on the phoneme are so strong for the individual that related ones in a foreign language are "heard" and "produced" as the native-language phoneme when the non-native speaker speaks the new language. For example, Arabic has the phoneme /b/ but no phoneme /p/. When speakers of Arabic are not fully proficient in English, they regularly pronounce the English /p/ as a /b/. Similarly, Arabic, unlike English, has several sounds in the "h" range (/h/, /ḥ/, and /x/). In spontaneous speech and conversation, native speakers of English who are learning Arabic often produce and hear all three as /h/. Aphasics too may suddenly appear to have what sounds like a foreign accent as the result of brain damage. This illustrates that the phonetic distortions associated with aphasia can be quite systematic in such a way that certain phonemes (or suprasegmentals) are particularly impaired, causing the "accent."

The foreign accent data also apply to notions of morphophonology, as words that are morphophonologically not permitted in the first language are particularly difficult to produce in the second language and are often betrayed by foreign accent at the impermissible points. For example, because words cannot start with a sibilant-stop-resonant cluster in Spanish, Spanish speakers will regularly add a vowel at the beginning of English words (e.g. "spring" is produced /ɛsprIŋ/).

Recall that when phonemic substitutions are made by aphasics, the substitutions are markedly more likely to differ from the phoneme that they substitute for by only one feature (such as voicing or frication) and markedly less often by two or three. Thus aphasic pronunciation of the word "cat" is more likely to be /kæd/ or /kɪt/ than it is to be /kɪs/. The notion of *distinctive features* – the linguistic constructs such as manner or place of articulation that distinguish among similar phonemes – is supported by such a pattern of breakdown.

The *syllable* is a familiar unit of theoretical analysis. The psychological strength of the syllable is manifested when both normal speakers and aphasics can demonstrate they remember the number of syllables in a word they cannot think of in the tip-of-the-tongue phenomenon. The further breakdown of syllables into less familiar units of *"onset"* and *"rhyme"* is plausible in light of another tip-of-the-tongue phenomenon, whereby aphasics, like normals, can sometimes remember the initial phoneme of a word they cannot remember in its entirety.

Suprasegmental phenomena are also attested to in the data from the populations we have considered. Recall that linguistic *tone* in speakers of tone languages appears to be easily discriminated from pitch patterns that are not linguistic. The evidence comes not only from laterality studies in normals, but also from observation of tone breakdown in patients with Broca's aphasia. Patients who have difficulty with intonation for syntax but not with linear pitch patterns provide evidence for the psychological reality of *intonation patterns* that serve syntactic functions.

The rule-governed relationships between the phonological forms produced by children with Specific Language Impairment (SLI) and those of normally developing children likewise testify to the notion of word-form principles in language acquisition. While age-matched children have already acquired a certain type of consonant cluster in a certain position, a child with SLI may systematically produce a reduced form of that consonant cluster (e.g. word-final /sp/ as in the word "clasp"). Both the ability of the normal children to produce the consonant cluster and the contrasting delay in the child with a specific language impairment (for whom the word "clasp" might be produced like the word "class") testify to the brain-based "psychological reality" of the constraints on lexical shape.

The fact that fluent aphasics and demented patients produce neologisms that invariably conform to the morphophonological constraints of the speaker's language is evidence for such morphophonological rules. A related set of evidence for real-word morphophonology derives from the fact that the demented patient HCEM (see chapter 8) would spontaneously correct deliberately inserted phonological errors in repeating back the words and sentences of her examiner.

Morphology

A certain psychological reality for the notion of *word* is seen in the fact that many agrammatic aphasics, when they delete affixes, only do so in such a way that real words in their language will be the outcome.

Word classes are seen as meaningful in production in several different ways. The distinction between functors and substantives is clearly manifested in the breakdown of the former but not the latter among agrammatic and paragrammatic patients. That *verbs* and *nouns* have special, independent status is seen in the relative dissociability of nouns and verbs among numbers of aphasics. In the aphasia chapters we discussed how some aphasics have nouns preferentially spared while others have nouns particularly impaired and verbs relatively spared.

The distinction between *affixes* and *word stems* is seen in their differential breakdown in agrammatism. Within affixes, distinctions between inflectional and derivational classes can be seen as well, not only in agrammatism but also in alexia (particularly deep dyslexia) and in dysgraphia (particularly in the errors of demented patients). As all these subjects produce word stems better than their affixes, we might assume that stems are simply better represented than affixes in the lexicon. Recall that fluent aphasics, by contrast, reproduce nonsense words with "appropriate" affixes so the dissociation is reciprocal; it is not simply the case that stems are more strongly represented and easier to access; rather the two types of elements are differentially organized.

People who acquire their first language in normal fashion often demonstrate the psychological reality of morphophonological rules by non-standard instances of adherence to them during their early stages of acquisition. For example, the child who overregularizes the past tense rules producing "doed" for "did" demonstrates internalization of that rule. Children's creative morphologizing can be seen as evidence for their linguistic analysis of the language they hear. For example, the child who asks (about what a magnet will attract) "What does this [mæg NET] to?," putting stress on the second syllable, shows that the stress assignment rule that distinguishes between pairs like *project* (N) and *project* (V) has been acquired and generalized.

In familial language impairment, the importance of morphophonological rules of affixation is made visible in that they break down. Recall that Goad and Rebellati pointed out how plural markers were realized by *compounding* rather than *affixation* in such individuals, and, as Gopnik has demonstrated, their SLT subjects can articulate rules for affixation but not apply them fully appropriately and automatically. Also, the general rules of compounding can break down in aphasic speakers as was reported of both German (Hittmair-Delazar, 1994) and Chinese (Packard, 1993).

That morphology itself can be dissociated from syntax is of interest. Recall the subjects with familial language impairment who had great difficulty with morphological markers of number, person, tense, and aspect but no problems with argument structure. Also, Miceli et al. (1983) have reported two Italian-speaking agrammatics, one of whom was impaired on morphosyntactic affixation but not on word order, whereas the other was impaired on word order but not on morphosyntactic affixation.

Syntax

The syntactic notion of *hierarchically organized phrasal units* appears to be determining where code-switching can take place in bilinguals. Zurif and Caramazza (1976) demonstrated that the ability to construct phrase-structure trees breaks down in agrammatics. Also, such concepts as our ability to appreciate syntactically *ambiguous sentences* (of the "Flying planes can be dangerous" type) are highlighted by the apparent breakdown of the ability to identify both interpretations of them in right-brain-damaged patients.

The importance of some notion of *complexity* of syntactic structure is seen by numerous reports across the populations studied that more complex syntax provides particular difficulties. This is seen in left-brain-damaged children as they recover, in Genie with respect to passive sentences as compared to active sentences, for example, and in agrammatics whose only comprehension problems, when any can be documented at all, are for more complex syntactic structures. The complexity of syntactic structures is often related to movement of constituents and the "traces" of that movement as we discussed in chapter 5. The "trace" itself has neither phonetic nor orthographic realization. In linguistic analyses the notion of trace has proved invaluable in explaining reference phenomena and the acceptability or unacceptability of many constructions. One kind of evidence for the reality of traces comes from the effects of this construct, posited for syntactic reasons, on phonology. For example, the question: Who do you want to visit? is ambiguous. The two possible answers are:

(1)   I want to visit Jean. or
(2)   I want Jean to visit.

However, it is only possible to use the colloquial "wanna" for sense (1) of this question. The contraction of "want to" to "wanna," is blocked on the second sense by the "trace" of the moved constituent "who":

YOU WANT TO VISIT WHO $\Rightarrow$ Who$_1$ do you WANNA visit t$_1$
YOU WANT WHO TO VISIT $\Rightarrow$ Who$_1$ do you want t$_1$ to visit

In the second underlying sentence, the trace between *want* and *to* prevents contraction. Grodzinsky has argued that it is sentences with traces embedded that pose particular difficulty for agrammatic patients to understand. If "traces" (as opposed to sentence length or number of arguments) can be shown to be the crucial factor in agrammatics' comprehension problems, this is consistent with their psychological reality.

The notion of *thematic role* – the relation a given noun has to the verb, e.g. subject, direct object, etc. – is also indicated in its apparent breakdown in agrammatic aphasia, as can be seen from such patients' error-prone performance on sentences with reversible passives. Agrammatic patients do not pick up the syntactic cues in a sentence like "the elephant was helped by the mouse" that indicate it was the mouse that was doing the helping.

A respected model of how sentences are produced is that of Merrill Garrett (e.g. 1983). Most crucial to that model is the notion that substantive lexical items like nouns and verbs are inserted into a sentence at a stage independent from that at which syntactic markers like inflectional suffixes are set into sentence frames. Garrett's model of processing syntax for production is given substantial support by the errors of sentence structure but not substantive lexical items in mild agrammatics, as well as the slips of the tongue of normals. That a separate level for *surface syntax* must exist is substantiated in the ability of demented patient HCEM to correct sentences to which errors of surface syntax have deliberately been added.

Lexicon and semantics

In linguistics there has been discussion of how words are "listed" in the internal lexicon. Are word-forms and their meanings dissociable? What other information is included with a lexical "item"? In particular it has been assumed that the characteristics of the words it must co-occur with, or those it can co-occur with are listed. Neurolinguists have, additionally, considered if there is more than one lexicon for the different modalities – one for written word forms to some extent distinct from the one for oral word forms. And psycholinguists and neurolinguists have asked how lexical items get "accessed," that is how they get "searched" when we need to "locate" them for use in a sentence.

That subjects, even aphasics, can distinguish real *words* in their language from words that are not in their language, is evidence for a certain psychological reality to the notion *lexicon.* It would appear that we indeed have at least one lexicon instantiated in our brain, with all the words we know in it.

Strong evidence for the reality of *lexical search* is our inability, sometimes, to find a word we are looking for. In anomic aphasics this phenomenon stands out as even more problematic. That it is the *form* of the word and not its *meaning* that is lost is evident from the fact that such patients can provide useful circumlocutions. In pure word-deafness, by contrast, patients recognize sound shapes of words as words in their language, but these "words" are divorced from the meanings. Such a double dissociation provides particularly strong evidence for the psychological reality of both systems of lexical organization.

The status of *word-class categories* and of *affix categories* as such has been dealt with above in the morphology section. It remains unclear whether affixable endings are listed in the lexicon with each of the words they can occur on or not. The current evidence suggests that inflectional affixes (like past tense *ed*) are unlikely to be listed with the words they may be appended to while derivational affixes (both prefixes like *ex* and *pre* and suffixes like *tion* and *like* in English) are likely to be.

Subtle differences in aphasic patients' abilities to name different categories of items have led to hypotheses about how the lexicon is organized in the brain. Semantic notions such as hierarchies of basic level words, particularly *subordinate* and *superordinate* words, may be seen to break down differentially, the reader will recall, in dementia. Severe dissociations between proper nouns and common nouns have been reported, between abstract and concrete nouns, and the related categories imageable and non-imageable nouns, and between mass nouns and count nouns (Grossman et al., 1993). A few highly educated aphasic patients have been reported to have formal speech spared, while informal, colloquial speech is more problematic. This is due, in part, to their lexical selections. Some theorize that it is word frequency effects that bring about these differences, but recently others have suggested it is the age of acquiring words, rather, that is reflected in such differential abilities.

The notion of *semantic networks* whereby related items are interlinked is evidenced by numerous forms of dissociated breakdown. Goodglass (1993), for example, has reported that aphasic patients often perform particularly poorly in comprehending body-part names. Hart, Berndt, and Caramazza (1985) have reported a patient with brain damage suffered after encephalitis, who had particular anomia for fruit and vegetable names. Specific anomia for animal names has been reported by Hart and Gordon (1992). Further evidence for semantic linking comes from the semantic errors of deep dyslexia and of deep dysgraphia (recall the patient who wrote "scissors" when asked to write "stapler"). That some type of form-based network also links words is evident by the fact that cueing by the first phoneme of a word helps access it (or in the case of demented patients, access other words that begin with that phoneme!). Further evidence comes from the finding that real-word substitutions in aphasics' language are often phonologically similar to the target words, both in speech errors and in dysgraphia (e.g. *eel* or *snake* for *snail*).

Pragmatics

Pragmatic phenomena break down in dissociable ways in patients with right-brain damage and those with dementia. The ability to appreciate non-literal aspects of language (such as humor or statements requiring inference) breaks down while literal aspects of language pose no problem for such patients. The ability of normals but not these patients to appreciate ambiguity in sentences and homonomy in spoken words suggests the dissociable breakdown of these language skills.

All sorts of *conversational rules* are "proved" in the breaking of them by demented patients. These include error repair, topic maintenance, and the like. Certain ones, by contrast, are maintained until relatively late, such as the ability to take turns and to maintain eye contact. The improper use of anaphoric pronouns among such patients is a striking example of their particular impairment in the ability to monitor what the interlocutor knows.

Grice's first three conversational *maxims* (quantity, relevance, and manner; see chapter 7) are vividly exemplified in their violation by demented patients who speak too much, tangentially, and in disorganized fashion, taking little account of what the interlocutor may fail to comprehend. Grice observed that the maxims reflect what listeners expect. When listening to patients in the middle-to-late stages of Alzheimer's disease, listeners find themselves befuddled by the breakdown of the conversation despite their best efforts. Only with a linguist's analysis (like that of Hamilton, 1994 a and b) can the specific components of breakdown be extracted.

With right-brain-damaged patients, by contrast, it is another set of pragmatic phenomena that strike the interlocutor as problematic, and thus strike the researcher as "real." The particular interaction of *emotional content* with discourse is evident in its problematic nature for right-brain-damaged patients, suggesting another distinct paralinguistic level that cuts across language, at least across lexicon, maturation, and discourse.

Language choice in bilinguals may be seen as a pragmatic ability that can independently break down. While this is rarely seen in aphasic bilinguals, it is particularly evident in demented patients who will inappropriately address an interlocutor in a language the interlocutor cannot understand.

Language structure inherent in written language systems

We believe that different types of orthographic systems will be related to differential use of brain space for written language representation. The differential breakdown of different orthographies in bilingual alexics is evidenced, for example, in the Hinshelwood study on the educated English man for whom reading classic Greek was best spared. The interface between phonology and those orthographic systems that link to it is made patent by the differential sparing/impairment of each. The Japanese orthographic system offers the opportunity, which some alexic patients demonstrate, to have either syllabic or logographic elements particularly impaired. The existence of such patients is evidence that the two systems make use of different mechanisms in reading.

The fact that some children who are learning to read find *decoding* words particularly difficult while others find *whole-word reading* particularly difficult (and similar breakdown can be seen in some adult brain-damaged patients) is evidence for *two* distinct *routes* in normal reading.

The importance of *spelling regularity* in a language like English (whose spelling system is ideal only for historical information about words and documenting such dissociations in breakdown!) can be inferred from the data from surface dyslexics in whom the distinction is manifest. Even demented patients have more difficulty with their spared reading aloud of irregularly spelled (as compared to regularly spelled) words, and will make regularization errors in their writing of them.

Conclusion

In this chapter, we have highlighted the various ways in which the dissociation of abilities in language breakdown parallels the division of linguistic and psycholinguistic phenomena into components for analysis. We have touched on some particular linguistic constructs and tied together evidence for their psychological reality from normal populations with new pieces of evidence from the language behavior of people with brain damage and from the normal populations mentioned in this book.

The frequent "fit" of linguistic theory with language performance in breakdown would suggest a well defined "map" of language in the human brain. However, the many articles cited in our chapters leave open countless questions for further research. Also, we must look for instances where the details of the data refuse to fit nicely into any theory. It is markedly easier to locate instances where linguistic categories fit the data than it is to claim that one has data which pattern in a way for which no linguistic theory to date provides an appropriate explanation.

12 The future of neurolinguistic study

Introduction

As we intimated in the introductory chapter, the science of neurolinguistics is currently in a growth-spurt. Researchers are joining the field from linguistics, speech-language pathology, psychology and neurology in increasing numbers. More papers are being published, in more journals than even five years ago. However, although knowledge is being expanded, no fully-refined theories to explain the relation of the language and brain phenomena we have detailed have yet been developed. Certain overarching concepts, however, have been accepted by the field, such as some distinction between language and non-language areas of the left hemisphere, and substantial distinction between left-hemisphere and right-hemisphere contributions to language abilities and performance. Where will the field go from here?

Linguistics

As the field of linguistics has progressed over the last decades, emerging trends have been profitably adopted by neurolinguistic researchers. Recent understanding of language includes an appreciation of the complexity of rule systems. Neurolinguists have begun to look for subtle linguistic difficulties even in patients for whom the "basics" of language (e.g. word order) are intact. Patients with impaired performance can now be tested in ways that reveal preserved competence (e.g. well-formedness judgment tasks). As our understanding of language breakdown becomes more refined, we might consider whether a linguistic theory is compatible with the data from language breakdown as one criterion for evaluating the linguistic theories.

Research in the linguistics and sociolinguistics of bilingualism has led to improved testing of bilinguals with language impairments. For example, several decades ago, all "language mixing" was considered inappropriate. Now, language-impaired bilinguals can be evaluated based on norms for their culture for bilingual code-switching. As our ability to measure language-processing times on-line continues to improve, this too will benefit neurolinguistic research. Not only will we be able to distinguish between frank breakdown of certain phenomena and sparing of others, we will also be able to discriminate between tasks that take longer than normal to perform and tasks that are performed at normal speeds. This will open up the possibility of a subtler set of dissociations that will give us new information about distinctions among linguistic entities as they are represented and processed in the brain.

Speech-language pathology

An area of interest that has engaged some researchers is devising and testing theory-driven forms of therapy for brain-damaged patients. The area is problematic because it is unclear that therapy based on linguistic, psycholinguistic or cognitive neuropsychological theory is any more effective than therapies devised by successful clinicians based on their unarticulated theories of how language-recovery works and their own sense of what is likely to work.

David Crystal (1981) was an early proponent on the field he calls "Clinical Linguistics"; his primary focus has been on childhood language disorders, but he also includes adult aphasias. The goal of clinical linguistics is to perform linguistic analyses in the assessment of the language-impaired patient to provide guidance in selection of the materials and goals of the therapy. Hypotheses are developed as to what the principal problems of the patient are. Treatment then focuses on the areas that have been deemed problematic. When the treatment proves useful, the hypothesis is considered to have been correct. Mitchum and Berndt (1991), for example, report the case of an aphasic who had great difficulty producing sentences. Their linguistic analysis of his problems suggested three symptoms that could be focused on: impaired retrieval of main verbs, problems with the grammatical morphemes associated with the main verb, and surface structure problems with the underlying thematic roles of verb arguments. The first therapeutic intervention they tried focused on making verbs available to the patient; however, even when they did so for a limited set of main verbs, his sentence production using these verbs showed no improvement. Then they focused, instead, on the patient's inability to appropriately choose auxiliary verbs and corresponding inflections on verbs. They hypothesized that the patient's problem was not strictly linguistic, rather, that it lay with appreciating the temporal nature of what was to be described. Showing the patient picture sequences indeed proved helpful in enabling him to generate fuller sentences.

While we would argue that therapy is an art form as least as much as a science, it would hardly seem appropriate to ignore the possibilities of using theoretical constructs in determining what aspects of the patient's language are impaired and how they might be worked on. To date, however, while such hypothesis-driven therapy has worked during the therapy session for a few individual subjects and led us to understand which stage of the language processing may be problematic for them, it has generalized no better than any of the more standard therapies. That is to say, even for the individual patient with Broca's aphasia, working on such a phenomenon as verb retrieval has not generalized to enable the patient to speak in complete sentences (Mitchum and Berndt, 1991). Moreover, it would be useful for such a process to permit us to work with larger groups of individuals and not just individual patients. The attraction of such an approach is that each speech-language pathologist is encouraged to be a scientist, that is, to theorize about what the patient's language problems are, develop hypotheses as to how to work with the patients on the problems, and to test whether their hypotheses are useful in helping patients overcome their problems.

The difficulty, as we see it, is that the theories that have been invoked in the field of speech-language pathology are linguistic and psycholinguistic theories. However, we maintain, it is psychological theories of learning (both normal learning, and learning after brain damage) that would be most pertinent to this project. While such psychological theories may be used in cognitive rehabilitation, a field that has developed to work with head-injured patients who lose social skills and attention and memory, such theories have not entered into the recent discussions of theory and therapy for aphasics.

In chapter 11 we mentioned theoretical constructs in arithmetic such as commutativity – the fact that the sum of A plus B when added to C equals A plus the sum of B and C. While the rule of commutativity may describe our eventual knowledge of arithmetic, there is no reason to believe it enters into how the facts of commutativity are best taught to us. Similarly, while it is hard to imagine that theories of language learning, both in normals and in brain-damaged patients, would embody principles that flatly contradict those of linguistic or psycholinguistic theories of grammar and its role in normal language processing, it is also conceivable that the crucial parameters are related at least as strongly to components of learning theory as they are to components of the abstract descriptions of language and its processing. In recent years linguists have developed the notion of learnability. Learnability adds the constraint on any linguistic rule that it must be structured in such a way that a child can learn it. However, this notion has been treated more in theoretical fashion and has not been extensively tested. Collaboration between developmental psychologists and, with respect to reading, education psychologists, should enhance linguists' understanding of the range of not only what is learnable but what is likely to be learned. Whether or not such notions of learnability in the child would apply to adults – aphasics or second-language learners – remains another question. Here again, educators, psychologists and neuropsychologists should provide useful approaches to complement the language-based ones of linguists and speech-language pathologists.

Artificial intelligence

A number of neurolinguists are excited about simulation of neural networks by computers. The cognitive scientists involved in "parallel distributed processing" approaches to neurolinguistics were mentioned in chapter 1 where we discussed connectionism. Precisely because such scientists as Kandel and his colleagues have demonstrated that neurons learn, these scholars have set up computer programs so that "layers" of units between an input stage and the output stage can "learn" to produce the correct output from a given input over time by changing the "weight" of the connections among them. Seidenberg and his colleagues have demonstrated that such computer models can appear to learn to read the same way children do, learning regular words more easily than irregular words, for example, and making the same sorts of errors that children make. Patterson and her colleagues have been able to simulate the patterns of reading breakdown in dyslexia by "lesioning" such models, that is, by rendering components of them either unable to operate at all or able to operate only more weakly than previously. Some scientists are quite optimistic about the possibility that such computer modeling will give us information about how the brain actually operates. Hinton (1992), for example, concludes his *Scientific American* article on learning by neural networks

> we still do not know which representations and learning procedures are actually used by the brain, but sooner or later computational studies of learning in artificial neural networks will converge on the methods discovered by evolution. When that happens, a lot of diverse empirical data about the brain will suddenly make sense and many new applications of artificial neural networks will become feasible. (p. 151.)

Others of us suspect that, while computers may indeed be able to simulate how brains operate once we know how they do, the likelihood that brains operate like computers is low. For one, computers – even ones set up to operate on parallel distributed processing principles – regularly incorporate efficiency as a governing assumption, whereas it is in the human's interest for brains to have redundant systems set up in case brain damage of one sort or another comes along. That such redundant systems are indeed available is evident from the neurolinguistic data on dual routes for reading, for example.

In our opinion, the future of neurolinguistics lies in four major areas, treated in separate sections below: The expansion of our knowledge of neurophysiological processing of language, the expansion of our knowledge of the way language relates to other cognitive abilities, the expansion of our knowledge of language breakdown in structurally various languages, and the continued development of brain-imaging techniques such as PET, MRI, and Evoked Potential to study event-related brain electric responses from the scalp (ERPs).

Neurophysiology of language

One of the most crucial prospects, as we indicated in the introduction to this book, that will dominate neurolinguistics in the not-too-distant future, is the study of the psychophysiological aspects of brain processing for language. The study of cellular contributions to learning and knowledge is still very basic (at the level of a snail with one or a few large neurons) and thus does not permit us much opportunity for making hypotheses about language organization yet. In recent decades Kandel and his colleagues have performed a series of experiments on the large cells seen in a snail called Aplysia (where humans have thousands of neurons governing our heart's spontaneous beating, this snail has four). They have demonstrated that two basic forms of learning come about through changes in the chemical environment that facilitates or inhibits electrical transmission from one cell to the next. These are habituation, in which the snail, like humans, learns not to pay attention to new stimuli that are not important, and sensitization, in which the snail, like humans, learns to pay particular attention to stimuli that are painful or otherwise important.

In humans, studies of the cellular level of brain neurophysiology of language are still a long way off. One of the hints we have that neurophysiology is involved, as it must be, in language is the fact that medications like bromocriptine facilitate language fluency in some aphasic patients (Albert, 1988, and Mimura, Albert and McNamara, 1995). More general influence of hormones on cognition has been seen in such studies as those by Buckwalter et al. (1993) and Henderson et al. (1992) in which they demonstrate that older women who have taken estrogen replacement around menopause appear to have spared naming abilities with advancing age, alongside a decreased risk of Alzheimer's disease. Kimura has also demonstrated hormonal influences on cognition. For men she reports seasonal variations in spatial abilities. In spring, testosterone levels are low and performance is up. Hampson studied women across the menstrual month and found that when estrogen is high, performance on articulatory tasks is high while that on visual/spatial tasks is low (Kimura and Hampson, 1994).

Such studies are the early entries in the study of the neurophysiology of cognition, a field which is likely to expand markedly in the coming decades.

The relationship between language and cognition

As our knowledge of the various populations discussed in this book is increasing, and as neuropsychological knowledge is generally increasing it becomes more possible to consider the ways in which language performance is influenced by non-language cognitive abilities. Recall that, with respect to SLI children, Tallal's theory has been that, at least for a substantial subset of children with surprising difficulty in learning to read, the problem lies with a slowdown of auditory processing. More general disturbances of attention have also been considered as crucial in dyslexic children's failure to learn to read (Whyte, 1994). A body of literature on the language changes associated with healthy aging, such as the lessened ability to draw inferences from paragraph-length text has suggested that these changes are associated with the generally slower processing that accompanies aging. Increasing memory problems associated with aging have also been linked to performance on recalling paragraphs and even remembering the names of items and people (e.g. Light and Burke, 1988). Friederici and Frazier (1992) tested whether verbal memory *per se* posed a problem for agrammatic comprehension. They posed an alternative explanation, that processing demands that are specific to syntactic structure render comprehension difficult for patients with agrammatic comprehension. More specifically, they focused on assignment of themes, that is, roughly, whether a given word is the subject or object of a sentence, and determined that it is not generalized verbal memory but rather structure-related processing demands that influence performance.

Another cognitive non-linguistic factor that seems important in how we process lexical items is the frequency with which we have seen or heard them. While word frequency has no place in linguistic theory, it figures strongly in psycholinguistic theory; the more frequent a word is, as a rule, the easier and/or faster it is to process. In recent years some researchers have raised the question of whether it is frequency *per se* that brings about this effect, or something closely related to it such as how familiar a word is, or how imageable it is, or even the age at which it was acquired. Hirsh and Ellis (1994) have used statistics to demonstrate that in the mild apparently anterior aphasic they saw, the naming impairment, whether by spoken naming, written naming, or reading aloud, was better explained by age of acquisition (with earlier items better spared) than by frequency. In a previous paper Hirsh (1992) had reported another case of a patient for whom the opposite was true, that is, word frequency was a better predictor than age of acquisition. Indeed Bradley's finding (Bradley et al., 1980) about agrammatic aphasics was striking because she observed that while they maintained the frequency effect for substantives as normals do, they also treated functors according to a frequency principle, which normals do not do.

In the study of agrammatism one of the underlying causes that has been posited is limited ability to compute meaning during language processing (Menn and Obler, 1990). Tesak (1994) tests the role of cognitive load by varying it along four dimensions: a semantic dimension (concrete vs. abstract words), a morphological dimension (simple vs. complex), a plausibility dimension (plausible vs. implausible), and a surface syntax dimension (short vs. long sentences). On several different tasks, the four patients with Broca's aphasia who were tested show more errors on tasks where the cognitive-load parameter is greater. When cognitive load is reduced, however, for example where functor words are highlighted for patients (Nespoulous and Dordain, 1991), we may see enhanced performance in reading them aloud by agrammatic patients.

The excitement of studies in this area is reflected in the expansion of new journals such as *Cognitive Neuropsychology*, whose focus is largely on language, and *Brain and Cognition* which complements *Brain and Language*.

Cross-linguistic studies

The third major recent expansion that seems likely to continue in neurolinguistics is the study of specific linguistic structures peculiar to one or several but not all languages that may break down in agrammatism. A team of researchers in Finland headed by Niemi and Laine (e.g. Laine et al., 1994) is regularly pushing back the boundaries of what we now know about agrammatic and paragrammatic breakdown in their highly synthetic language, while scholars of the highly analytic language Chinese are informing us about the ways in which breakdown occurs in languages with few inflections and few obligatory functors (Lu, 1994, and Packard, 1993). For example, in highly synthetic languages, where a word may, in principle, have as many as 15 affixes, most of these affixes are optional. Finnish-speaking agrammatics will omit virtually all optional elements, and thus speak in a relatively simplified structure, perhaps even substituting items within the paradigmatic slots in cases of paragrammatism, but without making frank errors (Niemi et al., 1990).

In Chinese, by contrast, there are few inflections and virtually all functor words are independent, unbound morphemes. Here one is more likely to see omission or substitution of these items in agrammatic and paragrammatic patients. Also, all optional functors will not be included in sentences. Consider the homophonous word *zai* that has two different functions: a locative marker and a marker of progressive aspect. The latter is markedly more impaired in agrammatics than the former (Lu, 1994), presumably because it carries less meaning.

One example of the use of language-specific phenomena to test theories is reported by Jarema and Friederici (1994). Precisely because French offers a minimal pair in the words *la* and *le*, which can each serve as both articles and pronouns, they are able to decide between a theory of preserved abilities to deal with gender in agrammatics, versus a theory that items assigned a thematic role in a sentence (such as the agent or theme i.e. the object) are spared. Indeed their five French-speaking agrammatics were markedly better at pointing to the appropriate picture, as compared to another picture chosen to draw their attention, when the article forms *la* and *le* were tested than they were when the pronouns were tested, suggesting that the ability to take on a functional role in the sentence ("theta-role assignment") is not what accounts for the sparing of certain functors.

Another example of spared morphological processing in aphasia is seen in compounding. Here German is a particularly good language to look at, since compounding is a highly productive contributor to the lexicon. Indeed, on a naming task in which a mixed group of aphasics was asked to name the pictured items as specifically as possible, all the different sorts of aphasics demonstrated they remembered the compound words, even when they made errors. The vast majority of errors for each group was either compound verbal paraphasias or compound neologisms (Hittmair-Delazer, 1994). Interestingly, when one or the other of the two constituent morphemes was omitted, this was most frequently the first item and not the second. Although one might have expected this morphological pattern to be particularly impaired among the Broca's aphasics (we are not told if any of them are agrammatics), in fact the striking pattern of results is quite similar among Broca's, anomic, Wernicke's, and even transcortical aphasics.

Bates and her colleagues design research to approach the questions on specific behaviors across languages chosen for the contrasting structures each permits. For example, in a set of studies, they have predicted that speakers of languages whose inflectional systems carry substantial meaning (like German where articles carry information about the number, gender, case, and definiteness of the nouns that follow them) will have these meaning-heavy functors or affixes better spared in processing by brain-damaged patients. They demonstrated that this is true through cross-language studies (Bates et al., 1987).

The motivation for these cross-language comparisons lies in the balance we will eventually need to create between universal principles of language organization and structures and/or systems set up to process language-specific phenomena. Careful linguistic descriptions are crucial to the study of such phenomena, as are techniques to extract the necessary data from aphasics who are themselves interested in using strategies to mask the problems they may have in producing language. Methodological advances in finding ways to elicit these language behaviors are provided by Goodglass and his students and influence the entire cross-language agrammatism project. For example, Berko Gleason and Goodglass have taken the lead in developing ways to elicit structures from patients that require minimal memory load and assure that they know the lexical item required, while not giving them the structures they are being asked to produce outright. One can test that patients recognize individual lexical items to be used in a sentence-completion task by asking them to point to pictures. Then the sentence-completion task is designed to verbally constrain the possible responses to the target word, and a picture of the event described by the sentence is included as well.

Brain imaging

As we stated in chapter 3, the technologies for studying neurolinguistic organization in brain-damaged populations have been developing over the years, as have those for studying language processing in healthy individuals (of whom there are more, of course). Localizationists take particular pleasure in the ever more refined instruments for imaging the brain areas that become active during linguistic tasks. Researchers with access to medical centers are excited about positron emission technology (PET) and the possibility that magnetic resonance images (MRI) can be photographed quickly enough to provide information about on-line processing of language. Many generations of these technologies – and others that have not yet won out – compete to provide us knowledge of language processing in normals and in the brain-damaged populations we have discussed in this book. Unfortunately they are still expensive enough to preclude common use. As discussed above, in recent years psycholinguists have taken evoked response potentials (ERPs) – a refinement of EEG (electroencephalographs) – to use outside of hospitals in psycholinguistic laboratories. As we mentioned in chapter 3 the multiple sensors that can be attached to the surface of the scalp permit some degree of localization for the language behaviors tested, and because they can be administered in psycholinguistic laboratories, the psycholinguistic sophistication of the stimuli and the tasks can be great.

Recall that Genie had been tested with evoked potential; in her case only two points were sampled in each of the left and right hemispheres. More recently, Neville and her colleagues have placed at least 14 sensors on the scalps of the subjects and tested more specific linguistic phenomena. For example, in Neville et al. (1991) the authors took advantage of the fact that evoked response potentials are particularly useful for observing when something startling happens for a subject. Subjects listened to sentences and had to judge whether the sentences were good sentences in English. For half of the sentences, the target word was anomalous, either syntactically ("The man admired Don's of sketch the landscape") or semantically ("The boys heard Joe's orange about Africa"). Within the syntactically anomalous sentences there were violations of phrase structure (e.g. . . . about films America), and two phenomena related to rules about extracting question words from noun phrases: specificity ("What did the scientist criticize Max's proof of?") and subjacency ("What was picture of printed by the newspaper?"). The researchers presented each sentence one word at a time in order to determine which word rendered the sentence anomalous (e.g. in the last sentence above, the word "picture" would be the anomalous point; in the previous sentence, it would presumably be "Max's").

Semantically anomalous sentences produced what experts see as a classic "surprise response" about four hundred milliseconds after exposure of the stimulus. Moreover, it was seen in both hemispheres of the brain and most strikingly in posterior areas. Interestingly, while two of the syntactic types of violation showed their greatest surprise responses over the expected areas of the left hemisphere (temporal and parietal lobes for the violations of phrase structure, and anterior regions for the violations of specificity), the subjacency constraint violations were evident quite early (200 milliseconds after the crucial word) and diffusely represented in both hemispheres of the brain. Because the different types of syntactic violations resulted in different electrophysiological responses, we may conclude that the varied syntactic structures have real-time processing correlates in the brain.

In a second study (Neville, Mills, and Lawson, 1992), the authors varied only the final word of some sentences to make them anomalous. Half of the anomalous sentences ended in content words and half in functors. The surprise responses were different between the two types of words; for the functor words, they were over anterior regions of the left hemisphere, while for the content words, they were over posterior regions of both hemispheres. (See their figure 6, page 250, in Neville et al., 1992.) Interestingly, a second experiment using the same materials for non-native speakers of English (in this instance, people born to deaf parents, whose home language is ASL and who did not learn English until they attended school) showed very similar responses to those of English native speakers for the written English content words, but substantially different responses for the written English functor words.

Conclusion

The elegant sophistication of language structures and those brain operations that must subserve them is enticing. Surely our language "map" of the brain is more correct than the phrenological map of Gall, but its shape is still shifting and the labels are not yet fixed. Moreover the two-dimensional notion of *map* will not suffice as an analogy for the future, as cortical topography is at best the surface component of a multidimensional set of systems – cortical linked with subcortical – that enable us to use language.

Those of us who choose the field of brain-language study choose it with the recognition that overarching truths may not appear in our lifetime, but that the areas we carve out for pushing back the frontiers will contribute to an eventual understanding of the ways in which the human brain enables human communication to take place.

Glossary

Abstract Attitude	Goldstein's notion of the ability to take initiative, make choices, link concepts, infer gists, conceptualize, etc., that is lost in some aphasic patients.
Affix	A morpheme (q.v.) that is "bound to" a stem (q.v.) to create a word.
Affixation	The process of binding a morphological item (usually a prefix or a suffix) to a stem, usually for purposes of inflection or derivation (q.v.).
Agrammatism	A symptom of aphasia whereby bound and free morphemes (q.v.) are omitted in speech production and/or writing.
Alexia	Reading difficulties resulting from brain damage in a previously literate person.
Analogy	The inference of some similarity based on an observed relationship. For example, a child might create the verb "magnet" from the noun "magnet" based on other two-syllable pairs like "project."
Analytic languages	These are languages, like Chinese, that use virtually no bound functors in their morphosyntax (q.v.).
Anterior	The front of the brain. The phrase *anterior aphasia* refers to the non-fluent aphasias associated with frontal lobe lesions.
Aphasia	Language disturbance resulting from brain damage.
Assimilate	The morphophonological process whereby one phoneme (sound) changes to be more similar to

an adjacent one. The word "assimilate" itself is an example, as it is composed of the Latin prefix "ad" meaning "towards" and the stem "simil" meaning "similar." The "d" of the prefix assimilates to the "s" to produce the word *assimilate* instead of *adsimilate*.

Autism
A childhood disorder due to unknown brain damage characterized by severe inability to relate to and communicate with others.

Axon
The extension of the cell which carries impulses away from the cell body.

Bidialectalism
The ability to speak two dialects, often a standard dialect and a non-standard dialect.

Bilingualism
The condition of speaking two languages with some proficiency.

Bound morphemes
Affixes that are part of a word.

Brodmann's areas
Subareas of cortex that have different cellular patterns, mapped by Brodmann in the nineteenth century. (See Figure 2.5.)

Central nervous system (CNS)
The system that includes neuronal structures in the brain and spinal cord, in contrast to the peripheral nervous system.

Circumlocutions
Multi-word responses that describe what brain-damaged patients want to say when they cannot remember the specific word, e.g. "those things you write with" for "pens."

Closed-class items
This word is synonymous with "functors" in neurolinguistics. It refers to the "little words" such as prepositions, articles, etc., that form a class of grammatical functors with relatively little meaning compared to open-class items such as nouns, verbs, and adjectives. They are called closed-class because it is extremely rare that items are added to this class in the historical development of the language.

Cognitive science
That field developing in the later twentieth century that studies cognition from a multi-disciplinary approach; the disciplines included are artificial intelligence, psychology, linguistics, computer science, and behavioral neurology.

Commissurotomy	An operation to cut all or part of the corpus callosum fibers connecting the two hemispheres of the brain. This operation is conducted to prevent the spread of severe epileptic seizures when no other treatment has been effective.
Competence	The linguistic notion that we have an internalized set of rules governing our language even when our production may be imperfect, for example, we may make speech errors.
Concreteness	Relying on literal interpretations, seen with right-brain damage, or in Goldstein's view, any brain damage.
Conduction aphasia	The form of language impairment after brain damage characterized by relatively fluent speech and good comprehension but particular difficulty with repeating phrases and sentences spoken by an examiner. (See Table 4.1.)
Connectionism	Around a century ago, this term referred to the school of neurologists whose model was a set of connected areas in the brain for different language abilities (e.g. speaking, writing). Currently it refers to theorists who assume that brain processes are not linear but rather carried out in parallel, as modern computers operate.
Corpus callosum	The set of fibers connecting the two hemispheres of the brain.
Cortex	The surface of the brain.
Cortical stimulation	The technique for determining the language area of the brain before surgery to curtail severe epilepsy. In this procedure the cortex of the brain is exposed and small points of it are stimulated with electricity; only when stimulation occurs within the subject's language area does the subject have difficulty naming items.
Critical period	The period during which the brain has the ability to learn something, especially language.
Crossed aphasia	Aphasia in a right-hander resulting from a right hemisphere lesion.
Decoding	A way of reading whereby the subject assigns phonemes (sounds) to graphemes (letters), thus getting to the sound-shape of a word analytically rather than by recognizing the whole word.

Dementia	Cognitive decline resulting from brain damage.
Dendrite	The extension of the cell that carries impulses towards the cell body.
Dependencies	Relationships between words in a clause.
Derivation	That form of affixation (q.v.) that results in the change of word class (e.g. the noun "substance" can become the adjective "substantial"; the word "worker" is derived from "work."
Developmental dyslexia	Severe difficulty learning to read in childhood despite the absence of frank brain-damage.
Dichotic listening	A technique to study hemispheric dominance for auditory materials in which both ears are presented with different information at the same time.
Discourse	Speech that is longer than sentence-length, often as in conversation or story-telling.
Dissociations	Instances in which one patient is particularly impaired for a certain behavior (A) while another behavior (B) is spared. This is consistent with the two behaviors being organized independently of each other in the brain. If at the same time another patient shows the opposite (B is impaired and A is spared), we have a double dissociation, providing stronger support for the independence of A and B.
Distinctive features	A linguistic term referring to something that makes the smallest possible important distinction. e.g., in English (and many other languages) voicing of the consonant is a distinctive feature; it distinguishes, for example, between the words "bin" and "pin."
Dysarthria	Difficulty with producing intelligible speech as the result of brain damage. In dysarthria, the problem is not a linguistic one but rather a motoric one; the patients cannot get the muscles necessary for speech production to work properly.
Dysgraphia	Difficulties with writing as the result of brain damage.
Dyslexia	Problems with reading as a result of brain damage.
Error repair	In speech we often correct our speech errors

	unconsciously; listeners, too, will ignore these error repairs.
Fluent	In aphasiology this term refers to speakers who have no motoric difficulty in producing speech nor any agrammatism. Their speech production is at the normal pace or faster.
Functors	See closed-class items.
Gang effects	Also called neighborhood effects. In current theories of reading, these effects are seen when clusters of words have similar pronunciation for similar sequences of letters. For example, the words *hint*, *mint*, and *lint*, etc. form a gang, and can be recognized faster than *pint* which is excluded from this gang as its vowel is pronounced differently.
Gestural language	Often called Sign Language. A full-fledged language that developed in a community of deaf speakers.
Global aphasia	The most severe aphasic syndrome, in which both production of language and comprehension of it are extremely impaired.
Grammar	The internal representation of a set of rules describing a language; generating all and only the sentences in that language. Grammar determines a speaker's ability (see competence) to speak and understand that language.
Grammaticality judgment	Native speakers' judgments as to whether a certain structure is possible in their language or impossible. Linguists use these judgments as data for constructing theories to test predictions made by proposed grammars.
Gray matter	The surface parts of the cortex that traditionally look gray when prepared as slices of the brain to be studied after death.
Gyri	The rounded external parts of convolutions on the cortex of the brain.
Hemisphere	One-half the brain, referring particularly to the surface cortical areas, as a rule.
Holism	The approach to brain organization and processing that takes the position that the whole brain, or substantial parts of it, are called upon for most behaviors of interest, particularly language.

Hyperlexia	The phenomenon seen in some autistic children (q.v.) whereby, despite the fact that they speak very little to other people, they learn (usually teach themselves) to read at a very early age, and read aloud quite well, with little indication of comprehension.
Ideographs	The units of writing in a system such as Chinese which do not represent phonemes but rather morphemes (q.v.).
Idiot savant	An autistic child who has one striking ability, such as the ability to play piano or compute what day of the week a certain calendar date will fall on in the distant future, or the ability to do extremely complex mathematical calculations in his or her head.
Inflection	A process of affixing (q.v.) that is used for verb endings in some languages (such as Spanish and French) substantially and in others less; (e.g. in English present tense the verb is only inflected for the third person, "walks," instead of "walk" for the other persons).
Input	The language that is heard or read by an individual.
Language area	That area of the (usually cortical) surface of the brain that is presumed to be responsible for language because, when that area is damaged (or stimulated electrically) problems with language arise. Brain damage to cortical areas outside that area do not cause language disturbance (see Figure 1.1).
Language choice	For bilinguals, choosing which language is the correct one to speak with the individual they are speaking to.
Lesion	Brain damage.
Lexicon	That part of language where word forms and their meanings (and perhaps, some information about how they combine with other words and morphemes) are organized.
Lobes	Major areas of each brain hemisphere: frontal, parietal, occipital, and temporal.

Localization	That approach to neuroscience that is interested in discovering which areas of the brain are involved in which processes.
Logographs	See ideographs.
Magnetic resonance imaging (MRI)	A form of obtaining images of the brain via reading how magnetic fields pass through it.
Metalinguistic tasks	Off-line tasks that require the speaker to use language to describe language. Classic examples are tasks such as clapping once for each sound (phoneme) in a word, or telling the two meanings of an ambiguous sentence.
Modularity	A theory in cognitive science (q.v.) that there are subprocesses in a given process that contribute to a major cognitive process (e.g. language) without interacting substantially among themselves; only the output of one is available as input for the next and there is no feedback to the first. This contrasts with a connectionist (q.v.) approach.
Morpheme	The smallest possible meaningful unit of a language (the word "girls" has two, "girl" and the plural marker).
Morphology	The study of the smallest possible meaningful units of a language: how they are structured and how they interact.
Morphosyntax	The study of how morphemes (q.v.), especially bound morphemes (q.v.), participate in surface syntactic forms.
Motor area	That area of the cortex, just in front of the Rolandic fissure, that is responsible for movements of all parts of the body.
Neighborhood effects	See gang effects.
Neologism	A nonsense word.
Nerves	Bundles of neuronal cells with specific functions.
Neurology	The study of the nervous system and its operation and breakdown in the human body.
Neuron	Nerve cell.
Neurophysiology	The study of how the brain operates in terms of cells and their chemical environment.

Neuropsychology	The study of how cognitive abilities are instantiated in the brain, and how they may break down.
Non-fluent	With respect to aphasia, including marked effortfulness in production and/or omission or substitution of functors (q.v.) and bound morphemes.
Normals	People who are not brain-damaged.
Off-line processing	See on-line processing.
On-line processing	Processing as it happens, as opposed to off-line processing which means considering a linguistic unit after the fact. Grammaticality judgment is an off-line task; listening to a taped narrative in order to indicate whenever a certain phoneme occurs is an on-line task.
Onset	In a syllable, the beginning consonant or consonant cluster. (See Rhyme.) In aphasia, when the stroke or other brain damage began.
Open-class items	Substantives, as compared to functors: Nouns, verbs, adjectives.
Paradigmatic	As compared to syntagmatic (q.v.); items that can fill the same slot are paradigmatically related. The words "boy" and "girl" are paradigmatically related, while the words "boy" and "runs" are syntagmatically related.
Parallel distributed processing (PDP)	That modern connectionist theory that neither words nor syntactic structures are actually instantiated in any given area of the brain, but rather they and many related ones are energized to a threshold and the one that wins out by going over the threshold first is activated.
Paraphasia	A speech error associated with aphasia and dementia in which one open-class substantive is substituted for another.
Performance	As compared to competence (q.v.), the actual language we produce.
Phoneme	The smallest sound unit that can distinguish two words.
Phonology	The study of sound patterns, especially phonemes (q.v.) and how they relate to each other.
Phrenology	That late nineteenth-century "science" associated

with Gall, that created a map to localize different personality characteristics.

Plasticity	The notion that in childhood the human brain is relatively able to reorganize itself after brain damage.
Positron emission tomography (PET Scanning)	A dynamic method of viewing images of the brain as it processes information.
Posterior	(See also anterior.) The back parts of the brain.
Pragmatics	(Study of) the use of language beyond the traditional study of phonemes, morphemes, and sentence-level syntax. Different definitions of pragmatics focus primarily on discourse or primarily on conventions of language use such as how we may speak formally or informally.
Prefix	Affix (q.v.) that precedes the stem of a word.
Psycholinguistics	The study of sentence processing.
Psychological reality	The notion that a theoretical construct enters meaningfully into brain operations.
Rhyme	(See onset.) In a syllable, the part that remains after the initial phoneme or consonant cluster.
Savants	See idiot savant.
Semantics	The study of meanings in language.
(Somato) sensory areas	The areas of the brain just behind the Rolandic fissure that are responsible for processing sensation as it comes in from other body areas.
Spinal cord	The spinal cord is the bundle of nerves running within the spinal column bones (vertebrae) permitting spinal nerves to connect the brain and peripheral areas.
Split-brain patients	Patients whose corpus callosum (q.v.) has been cut in order to prevent the spread of severe epileptic seizures.
Stem	That basic part of a word that may take affixes. The stem of "unnatural" is "nature."
Subcategorization frames	The requirements verbs have about their arguments. For example, "put" requires a direct object and a locative phrase. It is okay to say "She put the car in the garage," but not "She put" or "She put the car" or "She put in the garage."

Subcortical	The vast central structures of the brain beneath the cortical surface (see cortex).
Subjacency constraints	The requirement that two positions in a sentence be in a certain structural relationship in order for movement to occur between the sites.
Substantives	(See closed-class items.) The major content-bearing words in a sentence: nouns, verbs, and adjectives.
Suffix	An affix (q.v.) that is appended to the end of a stem.
Sulci	The valleys between the gyri (q.v.) of the cortex.
Surface syntax	The actual syntactic form produced, as compared to its deeper structure.
Syndrome	A set of phenomena that are likely to occur together.
Syntagmatic	(See paradigmatic.) Items which are likely to be linked together in a string.
Syntax	The study of the structures of sentences (see surface syntax).
Synthetic	A type of language in which stems have affixes attached and these affixes may contain more than one sort of information.
Tachistoscope	A machine to present information to one or the other visual field so quickly that we can be assured the information goes first to only one hemisphere.
Thematic roles	The linguistic notion that words in a sentence take on roles such as the "doer" (Agent) or the "done to" (Theme).
Topic maintenance	In conversation, saying something to continue the topic that is already under discussion.
Turn-taking	In conversation, appropriately following the rules for when and how one may contribute.
Typology	The study of clusters of languages that have similar morphological and syntactic processes.
Unmarked	The most usual form, that needs no modification to be understood or used appropriately (e.g. in some parts of the United States, if you order a coffee, what you get (the unmarked form) is coffee with milk; to get black coffee you need to specify "black" or "without milk").

Visual field	That area of what we see when we are looking forward to the right or left of center.
Visual-gestural language	(See gestural language.) More commonly called sign language.
Voiced/voiceless	This dichotomy applies to this distinctive feature (q.v.) that distinguishes phonemes in many languages of the world. It refers to voice onset time (q.v.) being before – in the case of voiced – or substantially after – in the case of voiceless – members of a phoneme pair. The sounds /p/ and /b/ are such a phoneme pair; the /b/ is voiced.
Voice onset time (VOT)	The time before or after the opening of the lips to make a stop consonant at which vibration of the vocal cords (voicing) starts.
White matter	(See also gray matter). Those parts of the brain that appear white when traditionally stained after death; these are most of the subcortical areas.
Wild child	A child who has been brought up with virtually no human interaction.

Notes and suggestions for further reading

1   Neurolinguistics

Caplan, D., *Neurolinguistics and Linguistic Aphasiology: An Introduction*, Cambridge University Press, 1987, chapters 1 and 2.
Springer, S. P. and G. Deutsch, *Left Brain, Right Brain*, San Francisco, CA: W. H. Freeman and Company, 1981.

2   The brain

[1] The description of human neuroanatomy is compiled from a number of sources all of which are listed in the References.

Bhatnagar, S., and A. Orlando, *Neuroscience Fundamentals for Speech-Language Pathologists and Audiologists*, Baltimore, MD: Williams and Wilkins 1994.
Kandel, E., Small systems of neurons, *Scientific American*, September 1979.
Kandel, E. and J. Schwartz, *Principles of Neural Science*, New York: Elsevier, NY, Second edition, 1985.
Kandel, E. and R. Hawkins, The biological basis of learning and individuality, *Scientific American*, 1992.

3   How we know what we know about brain organization for language

Caplan, D. *Neurolinguistics and Linguistic Aphasiology: an Introduction*, Cambridge: Cambridge University Press, 1987.
Stemmer, B. and H. Whitaker, *Handbook of Neurolinguistics*, San Diego: Academic Press, 1998.

4   Aphasia: classification of the syndromes

Goodglass, H., *Understanding Aphasia*, San Diego, CA: Academic Press, 1993.
Several chapters in M. Taylor Sarno, ed. *Acquired Aphasia*, second edn, San Diego, CA: Academic Press, 1991. In particular: chapter 2, A. Damasio's "Signs of Aphasia" (re aphasia syndrome classification); chapter 3,

H. Damasio's "Neuroanatomical Correlates of the Aphasias," and chapter 13, D. Aram's "Acquired Aphasia in Children."
Poizner, H., E. Klima and U. Bellugi, 1987. *What the Hands Reveal About the Brain*, Cambridge, MA: MIT Press.

5   Aphasia: what underlies the syndromes

[2] Not all agrammatics show the same pattern of selected impairment as DE. For example, Tyler et al. (1990) discuss a patient (BN) who exhibited an inability to integrate both derivational and inflectional bound morphemes into higher syntactic contexts.

In M. Taylor Sarno's book *Acquired Aphasia* (San Diego, CA: Academic Press, second edn, 1991): Blumstein, S. "Phonological aspects of aphasia," 151–180.
Caplan, D., *Language: Structure, Processing and Disorders*, Cambridge, MA: MIT Press, 1992.
Kohn, S., *Conduction Aphasia*, Hillsdale, NJ: Lawrence Erlbaum Associates, 1992.
Menn, L., M. O'Connor, L. K. Obler, A. Holland, *Non-Fluent Aphasia in a Multilingual World*, Amsterdam: John Benjamins, 1995.
    Also, to be up-to-date, check the journals *Brain and Language*, and, starting with the 1993 issues, the *Journal of Neurolinguistics*.

6   Childhood aphasia and other language disorders

Curtiss, S., *Genie: A Psycholinguistic Study of a Modern-Day"Wild Child,"* New York, NY: Academic Press, 1977.
Matthews, J., ed., *Linguistic Aspects of Familial Language Impairment*, special issue of the *McGill Working Papers in Linguistics/Cahiers Linguistiques de McGill*, 10: May/December 1994.
Spreen, O., A. Risser, and D. Edgell, *Developmental Neuropsychology*, New York, NY: Oxford University Press, 1984.

7   Right-brain damage

Gazzaniga, M., Right hemisphere language following brain bisection: a 20 year perspective, *American Psychologist*, 38, 525–537, 1983.
Caplan, D., *Language: Structure, Processing and Disorders*, Cambridge, MA: MIT Press, chapter 9, 1992.
Bloom, R., Hemispheric responsibility and discourse production: contrasting patients with unilateral left and right hemisphere damage, in Bloom, R., L. K. Obler, S. De Santi, and J. Ehrlich, eds., *Discourse Analysis and Applications: Studies in Adult Clinical Populations*, Hillsdale, NJ: Lawrence Erlbaum Associates, 1994, 81–94.

Brownell, H., H. Gardner, P. Prather, and G. Martino, Language, communication, and the right hemisphere, in H. S. Kirshner, ed., *Handbook of Neurological Speech and Language Disorders*, New York: Marcel Dekker, 1994, 325–349.

8 Dementia

[3] In the example of LB's speech describing his war experience, there is an example of omission of "out of us," part of an idiom, suggesting that even for collocations and overlearned expressions there is some lexical decomposition.

Bayles, K., and A. Kaszniak, with C. Tomoeda, *Communication and Cognition in Normal Aging and Dementia*, Boston: Little, Brown and Company, 1987.

Lubinski, R., ed., *Dementia and Communication*, Philadelphia: B. C. Decker, 1991.

Hyltenstam, K. and C. Stroud, Bilingualism in Alzheimer's disease: two case studies, in K. Hyltenstam and L. K. Obler, eds., *Bilingualism across the Lifespan: Aspects of Acquisition, Maturity and Loss*, Cambridge: Cambridge University Press, 1989.

9 Disorders of the written word: dyslexia and disgraphia

Lesser, R. and L. Milroy, "Lexical Reading Disorders" in *Linguistics and Aphasia: Psycholinguistic and Pragmatic Aspects of Intervention*, London: Longman, 1993, pages 72–76.

Dyslexia, chapter in Rayner, K. and A. Pollatsek, *The Psychology of Reading*, Englewood Cliffs, NJ: Prentice Hall, 1989, pages 393–436.

Coltheart, M., K. Patterson, and J. Marshall, eds., *Deep Dyslexia*, London: Routledge and Kegan Paul, 1980.

Patterson, Karalyn, J. Marshall, and M. Coltheart, eds., *Surface Dyslexia: Neuropsychological and Cognitive Studies of Phonological Reading*, London: Lawrence Erlbaum Associates, 1985.

10 Bilingualism

[4] Actually, the phonemes of any language will tend to have slightly different articulation depending on the phonetic environment in which they occur.

Albert, M. and L. K. Obler, *The Bilingual Brain: Neuropsychological and Neurolinguistic Aspects of Bilingualism*, New York, NY: Academic Press, 1978.

Paradis, M. Multilingualism and aphasia, in G. Blanken, J. Dittman, H. Grimm, J. Marshall and C.-W. Wallesch, eds., *Linguistic Disorders and Pathologies*, in Marshall, 1994, Berlin: Walter de Gruyter, 1993.

References

Albert, M. L., 1988, Neurobiological aspects of aphasia therapy, *Aphasiology*, 2: 215–218.

Albert, M., and L. K. Obler, 1978, *The Bilingual Brain: Neuropsychological and Neurolinguistic Aspects of Bilingualism*. NY: Academic Press.

Alexander, M.P., and M. A. Naeser, 1988, Cortical-subcortical differences in aphasia. *Language, Communication and the Brain Research Publications: Association for Research in Nervous and Mental Disorders*, v. 66, F. Plum, ed., New York, NY: Raven Press.

Aram, D., 1988, Language sequelae of unilateral brain lesions in children, in F. Plum, ed., *Language, Communication and the Brain*, New York, NY: Raven Press, 171–197.

Ardila, A., and M. Rosselli, 1993, Language deviations in aphasia: A frequency analysis, *Brain and Language*, 44: 165–180.

Ashcraft, M., 1993, A personal case history of transient anomia, *Brain and Language*, 44: 47–57.

Bates, E., A. Friederici, and B. Wulfeck, 1987, Grammatical morphology in aphasia: Evidence from three languages, *Cortex*, 23: 545–574.

Bates, E., B. Wulfeck, and B. MacWhinney, 1991, Cross-linguistic research in aphasia: An overview, *Brain and Language*, 41: 123–148.

Baum, S., 1989, On-line sensitivity to local and long-distance syntactic dependencies in Broca's aphasia, *Brain and Language*, 37: 327–338.

Bayles, K., and A. Kaszniak, with C. Tomoeda, 1987, *Communication and Cognition in Normal Aging and Dementia*, Boston: Little, Brown and Company.

Berndt, R., A. Haendiges, C. Mitchum, and J. Sandson, 1997a, Verb retrieval in aphasia: 2. Relationship to sentence processing, *Brain and Language*, 56, 1: 107–137.

Berndt, R., C. Mitchum, A. Haendiges, and J. Sandson, 1997b, Verb retrieval in aphasia: 1. Characterizing single word impairments, *Brain and Language*, 56, 1: 68–106.

Berndt, R. S., and L. B. Zingeser, 1991, Grammatical class effect in word production: Finding the locus of the deficit, *Brain and Language*, 41: 597–600.

Bhatnagar, S., and A. Orlando, 1994, *Neuroscience Fundamentals for Speech-Language Pathologists and Audiologists*, Baltimore, MD: Williams and Wilkins.

Blonder, L., D. Bowers, and K. Heilman, 1991, The role of the right hemisphere in emotional communication, *Brain*, 114: 1115–1127.

Bloom, R., 1994, Hemispheric responsibility and discourse production: contrasting patients with unilateral left and right hemisphere damage, in Bloom, R., L. K. Obler, S. De Santi, and J. Ehrlich, eds., *Discourse Analysis and Applications: Studies in Adult Clinical Populations*, Hillsdale, NJ: Lawrence Erlbaum Asociates, 81–94.

Bloom, R. L., J. C. Borod, L. K. Obler and E. Koff, 1990, A preliminary characterization of lexical emotional expression in right- and left-brain damaged patients, *International Journal of Neuroscience*, 55: 71–80.

Bloom, R. L., J. C. Borod, L. K. Obler, and L. J. Gerstman, 1992, Impact of emotional content on discourse production in patients with unilateral brain damage, *Brain and Language*, 42 (2): 153–164.

Bloom, R., J. Borod, L. K. Obler, C. Santschi-Haywood, and L. Pick, 1996, Right and left hemispheric contributions to discourse coherence and cohesion, *International Journal of Neuroscience*, 88: 125–140.

Blumstein, S., 1991, Phonological aspects of aphasia, in M. T. Sarno, ed., *Acquired Aphasia*, San Diego, CA: Academic Press, second edition, 151–180.

Blumstein, S., and W. Cooper, 1974, Hemisphere processing of intonation contours, *Cortex*, 10: 146–158.

Blumstein, S., W. Cooper, E. Zurif, and A. Caramazza, 1977, The perception and production of voice-onset time in aphasia, *Neuropsychologia*, 15: 371–383.

Blumstein, S., W. Milberg, B. Dworetzky, A. Rosen, and F. Gershberg, 1991, Syntactic priming effects in aphasia: An investigation of local syntactic dependencies, *Brain and Language*, 40: 393–421.

Boder, E., 1970, Developmental dyslexia: a new diagnostic approach based on the identification of three subtypes, *Journal of School Health*, 40: 1–23.

Bradley, D., M. Garrett, and E. Zurif, 1980, Syntactic deficits in Broca's aphasia, in D. Caplan, ed., *Biological Studies of Mental Processes*, Cambridge, MA: MIT Press.

Broca, P., 1861, Remarques sur le siège de la faculté du langage articulé suivies d'une observation d'aphémie, *Bull. Soc. Anat.* Paris, 6, 330.

Broca, P., 1865, Sur le siège de la faculté du language articulé. *Bull. Soc.*

d'Anthropologie, 6: 337–393.

Brown, J. W., and K. L. Chobor, 1992, Phrenological studies of aphasia before Broca: Broca's aphasia or Gall's aphasia?, *Brain and Language*, 43: 475–486.

Brownell, H., H. Gardner, P. Prather, and G. Martino, 1994, Language, communication, and the right hemisphere, in H. S. Kirshner, ed., *Handbook of Neurological Speech and Language Disorders*, New York, NY: Marcel Dekker, 325–349.

Buchwald, J., D. Guthrie, J. Schwafel, R. Erwin, and D. Van Lancker, 1994, Influence of language structure on brain-behavior development, *Brain and Language*, 46: 607–619.

Buckingham, H., and A. Kertesz, 1976, *Neologistic Jargon Aphasia*, Amsterdam: Swets and Zeitlinger.

Buckwalter, J. G., E. Sobel, M. Dunn, M. Diz, and V. Henderson, 1993, Gender differences on a brief measure of cognitive functioning in Alzheimer's disease, *Archives of Neurology*, 50: 757–760.

Butterworth, B., 1979, Hesitation and the production of verbal paraphasias and neologisms in jargon aphasia, *Brain and Language*, 8: 133–161.

Caplan, D., 1987, *Neurolinguistics and Linguistic Aphasiology: an Introduction*, Cambridge: Cambridge University Press.

Caplan, D., 1991, Agrammatism is a theoretically coherent aphasic caegory, *Brain and Language*, 40: 274–281.

Caplan, D., 1992, *Language: Structure, Processing and Disorders*, Cambridge, MA: MIT Press.

Caramazza, A., and A. Hillis, 1991, Modularity: A perspective from the analysis of acquired dyslexia and dysgraphia, in R. M. Joshi, ed., *Written Language Disorders*, Dordrecht: Kluwer.

Caramazza, A., and G. Miceli, 1991, Selective impairment of thematic role assignment in sentence processing, *Brain and Language*, 41: 402–436.

Charlton, M., 1964, Aphasia in bilingual and polyglot patients – a neurological and psychological study, *Journal of Speech and Hearing Disorders*, 29: 307–311.

Chomsky, N., 1957, *Syntactic Structures*, The Hague: Mouton.

Coltheart, M., K. Patterson, and J. Marshall, 1980, eds., *Deep Dyslexia*, London: Routledge and Kegan Paul.

Corina, D., H. Poizner, U. Bellugi, T. Feinberg, D. Dowd, and L. O'Grady-Batch, 1992, Dissociation between linguistic and nonlinguistic gestural systems: A case for compositionality, *Brain and Language*, 43: 414–447.

Cossu, G., and J. Marshall, 1990, Are cognitive skills prerequisite for learning to read and write?, *Cognitive Neuropsychology*, 7: 21–40.

Crystal, D., 1981, Clinical linguistics, in G. Arnold, F. Winckel, and B. Wyke, eds., *Disorders of Human Communication*, 3, Vienna: Springer-Verlag.

Curtiss, S., 1977, *Genie: A Psycholinguistic Study of a Modern-Day "Wild Child,"* New York, NY: Academic Press.

Dalalakis, J., 1994, English adjectival comparatives and familial language impairment, in J. Matthews, ed., 50–66.

Dalalakis, J., 1994, Familial language impairment in Greek, in J. Matthews, ed., 216–228.

Damasio, A. H. Bellugi, H. Poisner, and J. VanGlider, 1986, *Sign Language* aphasia during left-hemisphere amytal injection, *Nature*, 322: 363–365.

Davidson, C., and R. Schwartz, 1994, Semantic boundaries in the lexicon: Examples from Jamaican patois, *Linguistics and Education*, 7: 47–64.

Dennis, M., and B. Kohn, 1975, Comprehension of syntax in infantile hemiplegics after cerebral hemidecortication: Left-hemisphere superiority, *Brain and Language*, 2: 472–482.

De Santi, S., L. K. Obler, H. Sabo-Abramson, and J. Goldberger, 1990, Discourse abilities and deficits in multilingual dementia, in Y. Joanette and H. Brownell, eds., *Discourse Abilities and Brain Damage: Theoretical and Empirical Perspectives*, New York, NY: Springer-Verlag, 224–235.

Eng Huie, N., 1994, *Dissolution of Lexical Tone in Chinese-Speaking Aphasics*, Ph.D. dissertation, City University of New York, NY.

Fedio, P., A. August, C. Myatt, C. Kertzman, R. Miletich, P. Snyder, S. Sato, and C. Kufta, 1992, Functional localization of languages in a bilingual patient with intracarotid amytal, subdural electrical stimulation, and Positron Emission Tomography, presented at International Neuropsychological Society meetings, San Diego, CA.

Finegan, E., and N. Besnier, eds., 1989, *Language: Its Structure and Use*, San Diego, CA: Harcourt Brace Jovanovich.

Forstl, H., 1991, The dilemma of localizing language: John Abercrombie's unexploited evidence, *Brain and Language*, 40: 145–150.

Freud, S., 1891, *Zur Auffassung der Aphasien*, translated to English as *On Aphasia* by E. Stengel, 1953, New York, NY: International University Press.

Friederici, A., and L. Frazier, 1992, Thematic analysis in agrammatic comprehension: Syntactic structures and task demands, *Brain and Language*, 42: 1–29.

Frith, U., 1985, Beneath the surface of developmental dyslexia, in K. Patterson, J. Marshall, and M. Coltheart, eds., *Surface Dyslexia: Neuropsychological and Cognitive Studies of Phonological Reading*, London: Lawrence Erlbaum Associates, 301–330.

Fukuda, S. H. and S. U. Fukuda, 1994, Familial language impairment in Japanese: A linguistic investigation, in Matthews, 1994: 150–177.

Galaburda, A., and T. Kemper, 1979, Cytoarchitectonic abnormalities in developmental dyslexia: A case study, *Annals of Neurology*, 6: 94–100.

Gandour, J., S. Ponglorpisit, F. Khunadorn, S. Dechongkit, P. Boongird, R. Boonklam, and S. Potisuk, 1992, Lexical tones in Thai after unilateral brain damage, *Brain and Language*, 43: 275–307.

Gardner, E. D., 1968, *Fundamentals of Neurology*, 5th edn, Philadelphia, PA: Saunders.

Garrett, M., 1980, Levels of processing in sentence production, in *Language Production*, vol. I. *Speech and Talk*, B. Butterworth, ed., New York, NY: Academic Press, 177–220.

Garrett, M., 1984, The organization of processing structure for language production: applications to aphasic speech, in D. Caplan, A. R. Lecours, and A. Smith, eds., *Biological Perspectives on Language*, Cambridge, MA: MIT Press, 172–193.

Garro, Luisa C., 1992, *Lexical Access in Bilinguals: the Case of English-based Spanish Calques*, Ph.D. dissertation, Graduate School of the City University of New York.

Gazzaniga, M., 1983, Right hemisphere language following brain bisection: a 20 year perspective, *American Psychologist*, 38: 525–537.

Geschwind, N., 1965, Disconnexion syndromes in animals and man, *Brain*, 88: 237–294 and 585–644.

Geschwind, N., and A. Galaburda, 1985, Cerebral lateralization: biological mechanisms, associations, and pathology, *Archives of Neurology*, 42: 428–459.

Geschwind, N., and P. Behan, 1982, Left-handedness: Association with immune disease, migraine, and developmental learning disorder, *Proceedings of the National Academy of Science of the USA*, 79: 5097–5100.

Goad, H., and M. Gopnik, 1994, Perception of word-final consonants in familial language impairment, in Matthews, 1994, 10–15.

Goad, H., and C. Rebellati, 1994, Pluralization in familial language impairment, in Matthews, 1994, 24–40.

Goldstein, K., 1948, *Language and Language Disturbances*, New York, NY: Grune and Stratton.

Goodglass, H., 1993, *Understanding Aphasia*, San Diego, CA: Academic Press.

Goodglass, H., and E. Kaplan, 1972, *Assessment of Aphasia and Related Disorders*, Philadelphia, PA: Lea and Febiger.

Gopnik, M., 1990, Feature-blind grammar and dysphasia, *Nature*, 344–715.

Gopnik, M., 1994a, Impairments of syntactic tense in a familial language disorder, in Matthews, 1994: 67–80.

Gopnik, M., 1994b, The articulatory hypothesis: Production of final alveolars in monomorphemic words, in Matthews, 1994: 129–134.

Gopnik, M., 1994c, The auditory perception/processing hypothesis revisited, in Matthews, 1994: 135–141.

Gopnik, M., and M. Crago, 1991, Familial aggregation of a developmental language disorder, *Cognition*, 39: 1–50.

Green, D., 1986, Control, activation and resource: A framework and a model for the control of speech in bilinguals. *Brain and Language*, 27: 210–223.

Grice, P., 1975, Logic and conversation, in D. Davidson and G. Harmon, eds., *The Logic of Grammar*, Encina, CA: Dickinson Press.

Grodzinsky, Y., 1984, The syntactic characterization of agrammatism, *Cognition*, 16: 99–120.

Grodzinsky, Y., 1991, There is an entity called agrammatic aphasia, *Brain and Language*, 41: 555–564.

Grosjean, F., 1982, *Life With Two Languages: An Introduction to Bilingualism*, Cambridge, MA: Harvard University Press.

Grossman, M., S. M. Carveli, M. Stern, S. Gollomp, and H. Hurtig, 1992, Sentence processing impairments in Parkinson's Disease: The role of attention and memory, *Brain and Language*, 42: 347–384.

Grossman, M., M. Stern, S. Gollomp, G. Vernon, and H. Hurtig, 1994, Verb learning in Parkinson's Disease, *Neuropsychology*, 8: 413–423.

Haglund, M., G. Ojemann, E. Lettich, U. Bellugi, and D. Corina, 1993, Dissociation of cortical and single unit activity in spoken and signed languages, *Brain and Language*, 44: 19–27.

Hamilton, H., 1994a, *Conversations with an Alzheimer's Patient*, Cambridge: Cambridge University Press.

Hamilton, H., 1994b, Requests for clarification as evidence of pragmatic comprehension difficulty: The case of Alzheimer's Disease, in R. Bloom, L. K. Obler, S. De Santi and J. Ehrlich, eds., *Discourse Analysis and Applications: Studies in Adult Clinical Populations*, Hillsdale, NJ: Lawrence Erlbaum Associates, 185–200.

Haravon, A., L. K. Obler, and L. Gerstman, Cognate words in balanced bilinguals, presented at the American Association of Applied Linguistics meetings, New York City, March 1991.

Hart, J., R. S. Berndt, and A. Caramazza, 1985, Category-specific naming deficit following cerebral infarction, *Nature*, 316: 439–440.

Hart, J., and B. Gordon, 1992, Neural subsystems for object knowledge, *Nature*, 359: 60–64.

Hécaen, H., and M. Albert, 1978, *Human Neuropsychology*, New York, NY: Wiley.

Henderson, V., J. Buckwalter, E. Sobel, D. Freed, and M. Diz, 1992, The agraphia of Alzheimer's disease, *Neurology*, 42: 776–784.

Hier, D., W. Yoon, J. P. Mohr, T. Price, and P. Wolf, 1994, Gender and aphasia in the Stroke Data Bank, *Brain and Language*, 47: 155–167.

Hinshelwood, J., 1902, Four cases of word-blindness, *Lancet*, 1: 358–363.

Hinton, G., 1992, How neural networks learn from experience, *Scientific American*, September, 145–159.

Hirsh, K., and A. Ellis, 1994, Age of acquisition and lexical processing in aphasia: A case study, *Cognitive Neuropsychology*, 11: 435–458.

Hittmair-Delazer, M., 1994, Naming in German compounds, *Journal of Neurolinguistics*, 8 (1): 27–41.

Hughlings Jackson, J., 1878, On affectations of speech from disease of the brain, *Brain*, 1: 304–330; 2: 203–222, 323–356.

Hyltenstam, K., and C. Stroud, 1989, Bilingualism in Alzheimer's disease: Two case studies, in K. Hyltenstam and L. K. Obler, eds., *Bilingualism Across the Lifespan: Aspects of Acquisition, Maturity and Loss*. Cambridge: Cambridge University Press.

Jakobson, R., 1941, *Kindersprache, Aphasie und allgemeine Lautgesetze*, Uppsala: Universitet Arsskrift, translated, 1968, by A. Keiler as *Child Language, Aphasia, and Phonological Universals*, The Hague: Mouton.

Jarema, A. G., and A. Friederici, 1994, Processing articles and pronouns in agrammatic aphasia: Evidence from French, *Brain and Language*, 46: 683–694.

Joanette, Y., and P. Goulet, 1991, Text-level representations as one determinant for lexical retrieval and sentence production deficits in aphasia: Comments on L. B. Zingeser and R. Sloan Berndt "Retrieval of nouns and verbs in agrammatism and anomia," *Brain and Language*, 41: 590–596.

Joanette, Y., and P. Goulet, 1994, Right hemisphere and verbal communication: conceptual, methodological, and clinical issues, *Clinical Aphasiology*, 22: 1–23.

Johnson, J., and E. Newport, 1989, Critical period effects in second language learning: The influence of maturational state on the acquisition of English as a second language, *Cognitive Psychology*, 21: 60–99.

Joshi, R. M., and P. G. Aaron, 1991, Developmental reading and spelling disabilities: Are these dissociable?, in R. M. Joshi, ed., *Written Language Disorders*, Dordrecht: Kluwer.

Kaufman, R. and L. K. Obler, 1993a, Classification of normal reading error types, in R. M. Joshi and C. K. Leung, eds., *Developmental and*

Acquired Dyslexia: Neuropsychological and Neurolinguistic Perspectives, Dordrecht: Kluwer.

Kaufman, R., and L. K. Obler, October, 1993b, Visual errors in deep dyslexia are normal, Academy of Aphasia presentation, Tucson, AZ.

Kean, M.-L., 1977, The linguistic interpretation of aphasic syndromes: Agrammatism in Broca's aphasia, An example, *Cognition*, 5: 9–46.

Kehayia, E., 1994, Whole-word access or decomposition in word recognition in familial language impairment: a psycholinguistic study, in Matthews, 1994: 123–128.

Kertesz, A., and T. Benke, 1989, Sex equality in intrahemispheric language organization, *Brain and Language*, 37 (3): 401–408.

Kimura, D., 1993, *Neuromotor Mechanisms in Human Communication*, New York, NY: Oxford University Press.

Kimura, D. and E. Hampson, 1994, Cognitive pattern in men and women is influenced by fluctuations in sex hormones, *Current Directions in Psychological Science*, 3: 57–61.

Kimura, D., and R. Harshman, 1984, Sex differences in brain organization for verbal and non-verbal functions, *Progress in Brain Research*, 61: 423–441.

Kimura, P., 1983, Sex differences in cerebral organization for speech and praxis functions, *Canadian Journal of Psychology*, 37 (1): 19–35.

Kohn, S., 1984, The nature of the phonological deficit in conduction aphasia, *Brain and Language*, 23: 97–115.

Kohn, S., 1992, *Conduction Aphasia*, Hillsdale, NJ: Lawrence Erlbaum Associates.

Laine, M., J. Niemi, P. Koivuselkä-Sallinen, E. Ahlsen, and J. Hyöenä, 1994, A neurolinguistic analysis of morphological deficits in a Finnish-Swedish bilingual aphasic, *Clinical Linguistics and Phonetics*, 8: 177–200.

Lassen, A., H. Ingvar, and E. Skinhoj, 1987, Brain function and blood flow, *Scientific American*.

Lenneberg, E. H., 1967, *Biological Foundations of Language*, New York, NY: Wiley.

Lesser, R., and L. Milroy, 1993, *Linguistics and Aphasia: Psycholinguistic and Pragmatic Aspects of Intervention*, London: Longman.

Lichtheim, L., 1885, On aphasia, *Brain*, 7: 433–84.

Light, L., and D. Burke, 1988, Patterns of language and memory in old age, in L. Light, and D. Burke, eds., *Language, Memory, and Aging*, New York, NY: Cambridge University Press, 244–272.

Linebarger, M., M. Schwartz, and E. Saffran, 1983, Grammaticality judgments in agrammatic aphasia, *Cognition*, 13: 361–379.

Lu, L., 1994, *Agrammatism in Chinese*, Doctoral dissertation, Boston University School of Medicine.

Lubinski, R., ed., 1991, *Dementia and Communication*, Philadelphia, PA: B. C. Decker.

Luria, A., 1973, Two basic kinds of aphasic disorders, *Linguistics*, 115: 57–66.

Mahecha, N., L. K. Obler, A. Haravon, and J. Centeno, 1992, Is there a bilingual monitor for code-switching?, presented at the Boston University Language Development Conference, October.

Masterson, J., M. Coltheart, and P. Meara, 1985, Surface dyslexia in a language without irregularly spelled words, in K. Patterson, J. Marshall, and M. Coltheart, eds., *Surface Dyslexia: Neuropsychological and Cognitive Studies of Phonological Reading*, London: Lawrence Erlbaum Associates, 215–223.

Mateer, C., S. Polen, G. Ojemann, and A. Wyler, 1982, Cortical localization of finger spelling and oral language: A case study, *Brain and Language*, 17: 46–57.

Mathews, P., L. K. Obler, and M. Albert, 1994, Wernicke and Alzheimer on the language disturbances of aphasia and dementia, *Brain and Language*, 46: 439–462.

Matthews, J., ed., 1994, *Linguistic Aspects of Familial Language Impairment*, special issue of the *McGill Working Papers in Linguistics/Cahiers Linguistiques de McGill*, 10.

McGlone, J., 1977, Sex differences in the cerebral organization of verbal functions in patients with unilateral brain lesions, *Brain*, 100: 775–793.

Macnamara, J., 1967, The bilingual's linguistic performance: A psychological overview, *Journal of Social Issues*, 23: 58–77.

McNamara, P., L. K. Obler, R. Au, R. Durso, and M. L. Albert, 1992, Speech monitoring skills in Alzheimer's Disease, Parkinson's Disease, and normal aging, *Brain and Language*, 42: 38–51.

Menn, L., and L. K. Obler, 1990, Cross-language data and theories of agrammatism, in L. Menn and L.K. Obler, eds., *Agrammatic Aphasia: A Cross-Language Narrative Sourcebook*, Amsterdam: John Benjamins Publishing Company, 1369–1389.

Miceli, M., A. Mazzucchi, L. Menn, and H. Goodglass, 1983, Contrasting cases of Italian agrammatic aphasia without comprehension disorder, *Brain and Language*, 19: 65–97.

Miceli, G., M. C. Silveri, C. Romani, and A. Caramazza, 1989, Variation in the pattern of omissions and substitutions of grammatic morphemes in the spontaneous speech of so-called agrammatic patients, *Brain and*

Language, 36: 447–492.

Mills, D. L., S. A. Coffey-Corina, and H. J. Neville, 1993, Language acquisition and cerebral specialization in 20 month-old infants, *Journal of Cognitive Neuroscience*, 5: 317–334.

Mimura, M., M. L. Albert, and P. McNamara, 1995, Toward a pharmacotherapy for aphasia, in H. Kirshner, ed., *Handbook of Neurological Speech and Language Disorders*, New York, NY: Dekker, 465–482.

Minkowski, M., 1927, Klinischer Beitrag zur Aphasie bei Polyglotten, speziel im Hinblick auf Schweizerdeutsch. *Schweizer Archiv für Neurologie und Psychiatrie*, 21: 43–72.

Mitchum, C., and R. S. Berndt, 1991, Verb retrieval and sentence construction: effects of targeted intervention, in G. Humphreys and M. Riddoch, eds., *Cognitive Neuropsychology and Cognitive Rehabilitation*, London: Lawrence Erlbaum Associates.

Mitchum, C., and R. Berndt, 1992, Clinical linguistics, cognitive neuropsychology and aphasia therapy, *Clinical Linguistics and Phonetics*, 6: 3–10.

Monrad-Krohn, G., 1947, Disprosody or altered "melody of language", *Brain*, 70: 405–415.

Morton, J., 1979, Word recognition, in J. Morton and J. Marshall, eds., *Psycholinguistics*, vol. 2, London: Elek.

Nespoulous, J.-L., and M. Dordain, 1991, Variability, attentional factors and the processing of grammatical morphemes in sentence production by an agrammatic patient, *Grazer Linguistische Studien: Neuro- und Patholinguistik*, 35: 33–45.

Neville, H., D. Mills, and D. Lawson, 1992, Fractionating language: Different neural subsystems with different sensitive periods, *Cerebral Cortex*, 2: 244–258.

Neville, H., J. Nicol, A. Barss, K. Forster, and M. Garrett, 1991, Syntactically based sentence processing classes: Evidence from event-related brain potentials, *Journal of Cognitive Neuroscience*, 3: 151–165.

Neville, H., S. Coffey, P. Holcomb, and P. Tallal, 1993, The neurobiology of sensory and language processing in language-impaired children, *Journal of Cognitive Neuroscience*, 5: 235–253.

Niemi, J., M. Laine, R. Hänninen, and P. Koivuselkä-Sallinen, 1990, Agrammatism in Finnish: Two case studies, in L. Menn and L. K. Obler, eds., *Agrammatic Aphasia: A Cross-Language Narrative Sourcebook*, Amsterdam: John Benjamins Publishing Company.

Nishimura, M., 1986, Intrasentential code-switching: The case of language assignment, in J. Vaid, ed., *Language Processing in Bilinguals: Psycholinguistic and Neuropsychological Perspectives*, Hillsdale, NJ: Lawrence Erlbaum Associates.

Novoa, L., D. Fein, and L. K. Obler, 1988, Talent in foreign languages: A case study, in L. K. Obler and D. Fein, eds., *The Exceptional Brain: Neuropsychology of Talent and Special Abilities*, New York, NY: Guilford, 294–302.

Obler, L. K., 1982, The parsimonious bilingual, in L. K. Obler and L. Menn, eds., *Exceptional Language and Linguistics*, New York, NY: Academic Press, 339–346.

Obler, L. K., 1983, Language dysfunction and brain organization in dementia, in S. Segalowitz, ed., *Language Functions and Brain Organization*, New York, NY: Academic Press.

Obler, L. K., and M. Albert, 1977, Influence of aging on recovery from aphasia in polyglots. *Brain and Language*, 4: 460–463.

Obler, L. K., and L. Menn, eds., 1982, *Exceptional Language and Linguistics*, New York, NY: Academic Press.

Obler, L. K., J. Cummings, and M. Albert, Subcortical dementia: Speech and language functions, presented at the American Geriatrics Society Meetings, Washington, DC., April, 1980.

Obler, L. K., B. Zatorre, L. Galloway, and J. Vaid, 1982, Cerebral lateralization in bilinguals: Methodological issues, *Brain and Language*, 15: 40–54.

Ojemann, G., and H. A. Whitaker, 1978, The bilingual brain, *Archives of Neurology*, 35: 409–412.

Packard, J., 1993, *A Linguistic Investigation of Aphasic Chinese Speech*, Dordrecht: Kluwer.

Paradis, M., 1993, Multilingualism and aphasia, in G. Blanken, J. Dittman, H. Grimm, J. Marshall, and C.-W. Wallesch, eds., *Linguistic Disorders and Pathologies*, Berlin: Walter de Gruyter.

Paradis, M., and M. Gopnik, 1994, Compensatory strategies in familial language impairment, in Matthews, 1994: 142–149.

Parkin, A. J., 1993, Progressive aphasia without dementia – A clinical and cognitive neuropsychological analysis, *Brain and Language*, 44: 201–220.

Pate, D., E. Saffran, and N. Morton, 1987, Specifying the locus of impairment in conduction aphasia, *Language and Cognitive Processes*, 2: 43–81.

Patterson, K., J. Marshall, and M. Coltheart, 1985, eds., *Surface Dyslexia: Neuropsychological and Cognitive Studies of Phonological Reading*, London: Lawrence Erlbaum Associates.

Patterson, K., N. Graham, and J. Hodges, 1994, Reading in dementia of the Alzheimer's type: A preserved ability? *Neuropsychology*, 8, 395–407.

Penfield, W., and L. Roberts, 1959, *Speech and Brain Mechanisms*, Princeton, NJ: Princeton University Press.

Pitres, A., 1895, Etude sur l'aphasie, *Revue de Médecine*, 15: 873–899.

Poizner, H., and R. Battison, 1979, Cerebral asymmetry and sign language: clinical and experimental studies, *Language*, 13: 58–77.

Poizner, H., E. Klima, and U. Bellugi, 1987, *What the Hands Reveal About the Brain*, Cambridge, MA: MIT Press.

Poplack, S., 1981, Syntactic structure and social function of code-switching, in R. Duràn, ed., *Latino Discource and Communicative Behavior*, Norwood, NJ: Ablex, 169–184

Poplack, S., S. Wheeler and A. Westwood, 1987, Distinguishing language contact phenomena: Evidence from Finnish–English bilingualism, in P. Lilius and M. Saari, eds., *The Nordic Languages and Modern Linguistics*, Helsinki: Helsinki University Press, 33–56.

Rayner, K., and A. Pollatsek, 1989, *The Psychology of Reading*, Englewood Cliffs, NJ: Prentice Hall.

Rosen, G., G. Sherman, and A. Galaburda, 1993, Dyslexia and brain pathology: Experimental animal models, in A. Galaburda, ed., *Dyslexia and Development: Neurobiological Aspects of Extra-Ordinary Brains*, Cambridge, MA: Harvard University Press.

Ruiz, A., A. Ansaldo, and A.R. Lecours, 1994, Two cases of deep dyslexia in unilingual Hispanophone aphasics, *Brain and Language*, 46: 245–256.

Sarno, J., L. Swisher, and M. T. Sarno, 1969, Aphasia in a congenitally deaf man, *Cortex*, 5: 398–414.

Sarno, M. Taylor, A. Buonoguro, and E. Levita, 1985, Gender and recovery from aphasia after stroke, *Journal of Nervous and Mental Disease*, 173: 605–609.

Sarno, M. Taylor, ed., 1991, *Acquired Aphasia*, second edn, San Diego, CA: Academic Press.

Satz, P., E. Strauss, and H. Whitaker, 1990, The ontogeny of hemispheric specialization: Some old hypotheses revisited, *Brain and Language*, 38: 596–614.

Schneiderman, E., and J. D. Saddy, 1988, A linguistic deficit resulting from right-hemisphere damage, *Brain and Language*, 34: 38–53.

Schneiderman, E., and C. Desmarais, 1988, The talented language learner: Some preliminary findings, *Second Language Research*, 4: 91–109.

Schwartz, M., O. Marin, and E. Saffran, 1979, Dissociations of language function in dementia: A case study, *Brain and Language*, 7: 277–306.

Shankweiler, D., S. Crain, P. Gorrell, and B. Tuller, 1989, Reception of language in Broca's aphasia, *Language and Cognitive Processes*, 4 (1): 1–33.

Sidman, R. L., and M. Sidman, 1965, *Neuroanatomy: A Programmed Text*, Boston, MA: Little, Brown.

Smith, N., and I. M. Tsimpli, 1991, Linguistic modularity? A case study of a "savant" linguist, *Lingua*, 84: 315–351.

Spreen, O., A. Risser, and D. Edgell, 1984, *Developmental Neuropsychology*, New York, NY: Oxford University Press.

Springer, S. P., and G. Deutsch, 1981, *Left Brain, Right Brain*, San Francisco, CA: W. H. Freeman and Company.

Stevens, S. J., 1991, Differentiating the language disorder in dementia from dysphasia – The potential of a screening test, *European Journal of Disorders of Communication*, 27 (4): 275–288.

Strong, O., and A. Elwyn, 1959, *Human Neuroanatomy*, Baltimore: The Williams and Wilkins Company.

Tallal, P., 1980, Auditory temporal perception, phonics and reading disabilities in children, *Brain and Language*, 9: 182–198.

Tesak, J., 1994, Cognitive load and the processing of grammatical items, *Journal of Neurolinguistics*, 8: 43–48.

Tyler, L. K., 1988, Spoken language comprehension in a fluent aphasic patient, *Cognitive Neuropsychology*, 5 (3): 375–400.

Tyler, L. K., and H. Cobb, 1987, Processing bound grammatical morphemes in context: The case of an aphasic patient, *Language and Cognitive Processes*, 2: 245–262.

Ullman, M., and M. Gopnik, Past tense production: Regular, irregular and nonsense verbs, in Matthews, 1994: 81–118.

Vaid, J., 1983, Bilingualism and brain lateralization, in S. Segalowitz, ed., *Language Function and Brain Organization*, New York, NY: Academic Press, 315–339.

Vaid, J., and D. Carina, 1989, Visual field asymmetries in numerical size comparisons of digits, words, and signs, *Brain and Language*, 36: 117–126.

Van Lancker, D., and V. Fromkin, 1973, Hemispheric specialization for pitch and "tone": Evidence from Thai, *Phonetica*, 1–109.

Von Economo, C., 1929, *The Cytoarchitechtronics of the Cerebral Cortex*, Oxford: Oxford University Press.

Wernicke, C., 1874, *Der aphasische Symptomencomplex*, Breslau, Poland: M. Cohn und Weigert.

Whitaker, Hai, 1976, A case of isolation of the language function, in H. Whitaker and H. Whitaker, eds., *Studies in Neurolinguistics*, vol. 2, New York, NY: Academic Press.

Whyte, J., 1994, Attentional processes and dyslexia, *Cognitive Neuropsychology*, 11: 99–116.

Wimmer, H., 1993, Characteristics of developmental dyslexia in a regular writing system, *Applied Psycholinguistics*, 14: 1–33.

Wuillemin, D., and B. Richardson, 1994, Right hemisphere involvement in processing later-learned languages in multilinguals, *Brain and Language*, 46: 620–636.

Yamada, J., 1990, *Laura: A Case for the Modularity of Language*, Cambridge, MA: MIT Press.

Yin, W., and B. Butterworth, 1992, Deep and surface dyslexia in Chinese, in H. Chen and O. Tzeng, eds., *Language Processing in Chinese*, New York, NY: Elsevier.

Zaidel, E., and A. M. Peters, 1981, Phonological encoding and ideographic reading by the disconnected right hemisphere: Two case studies, *Brain and Language*, 14 (2): 205–234.

Zingeser, L., and R. S. Berndt, 1990, Retrieval of nouns and verbs in agrammatism and anomia, *Brain and Language*, 39: 14–32.

Zurif, E., and A. Caramazza, 1976, Psycholinguistic structures in aphasia: Studies in syntax and semantics, in H. A. Whitaker and H. A. Whitaker, eds., *Studies in Neurolinguistics*, vol. 1, New York, NY: Academic Press.

Author index

Subject index